New forms
of work organisation
2

German Democratic Republic
India
Italy
USSR
Economic costs and benefits

International Labour Office   Geneva

ISBN 92-2-102110-6 (limp cover)
ISBN 92-2-102109-2 (hard cover)

First published 1979

Printed by Icobulle, 1630 Bulle, Switzerland

PREFACE

This is the second volume of a series devoted by the International Labour Office to the subject of new forms of work organisation. Thus in addition to a first volume* containing monographs concerning Denmark, Norway, Sweden, France, the Federal Republic of Germany, the United Kingdom and the United States, the Office is now publishing national monographs concerning the German Democratic Republic, India, Italy and the USSR, together with a paper on achievements and possibilities with regard to the evaluation of the economic costs and benefits of new forms of work organisation.

As already indicated in the Preface to the first volume, some of the national monographs have been prepared by independent research workers, and others by specialists attached to official bodies. Although a common outline was developed before the monographs were written, they are very different indeed not only in their arrangement but in their treatment of the subject of the organisation of work and its relationship to national political, social and economic institutions. The views put forward may be challenged, from different points of view, in government, business, union or academic circles. Without necessarily endorsing the opinions expressed in the monographs, the Office has deemed it worth while to publish these papers in order to show how different research workers and specialists attached to official bodies see the subject in different countries.

---

* ISBN 92-2-101991-8 (limp cover); ISBN 92-2-102005-3 (hard cover).

CONTENTS

GERMAN DEMOCRATIC REPUBLIC

GERMAN DEMOCRATIC REPUBLIC
Heinz Hanspach and Arno Schäfer*

SCIENTIFIC ORGANISATION OF WORK

In the German Democratic Republic the organisation of work is determined by the fundamental characteristics of socialist society. Political power, lying entirely in the hands of urban and rural workers, rests on the socialist ownership of the means of production and on socialist production relations. The right to work is guaranteed by the Constitution. All the endeavours of socialist society are centred on man and the development of a socialist personality. At every stage of social and economic development the activities of the socialist State, which co-operates closely with the trade unions, are focused on working people. Socialist democracy takes the form, in particular, of direct participation by the workers in the planning and direction of production.

The purpose of economic activity is to improve the satisfaction of the workers' material and cultural needs and to ensure personal fulfilment. The rapid development of production, scientific and technical progress and increasing efficiency and labour productivity all serve that purpose. The economy is moving steadily forward under the thrust of improved performance.

The scientific organisation of work is a system applied under the leadership of government departments, by agreement with the Confederation of Free German Trade Unions and its industrial sections. The system is applied not only in the production of goods but in services, administration and in the fields of education and health, with the co-operation of the workers concerned and under the responsibility of the managers of undertakings and the directors of other institutions.

The organisation of work is based on legislation, representation through the trade unions and the creative endeavours of the workers engaged in socialist emulation. Plans governing the organisation of work are made at various levels, from government departments to individual undertakings. Continuing improvements in the organisation of work are agreed upon at the level of the

---

* Respectively Director of the Central Labour Research Institute in Dresden and head of the division of scientific organisation of work in the State Secretariat for Labour and Wages of the Council of Ministers. The authors were assisted by Mr. Wolfgang Oese, scientific secretary in the Central Labour Research Institute.

undertaking through collective agreements between the union leadership and the management.

Aim und purpose

In the German Democratic Republic the scientific organisation of work serves exclusively human ends. Its purpose is to achieve the most acceptable form of work itself, the best working environment and the best labour relations, by making full use of scientific knowledge and of the workers' experience with a view to facilitating and enriching people's work and life.

All conditions of work are examined from the point of view of their influence on working capacity, on physical and mental well-being and on social welfare. The organisation of work is bound up with technology and with production engineering and management; it embraces the design of jobs, of the working environment, of labour relations and of material and moral incentives. It affects production proper as well as the preparation of production, management, administration and non-material aspects of national life.

The aim is to create conditions of work that will permit high output, promote the general development of the workers and help to foster socialist relations within the workforce of undertakings. The scientific organisation of work promotes this aim through restructuring and the redesign of existing processes as well as through the development of new machines, technology and workplaces; it is directed at the joint development of scientific, technical and social progress, and harmonises the interests of the individual, the staff of an undertaking, and society as a whole.

It relies on planning, the creativity of the workers and the teachings of science and technology. The improvements are not confined to questions of organisation and technology: an attempt is made to secure a constant extension of the workers' field of activity, to foster their development, to improve the creative aspect of the work, and to provide safe employment in an educational atmosphere.

Whether in society as a whole or at the level of the undertaking, improvements in work organisation are based on the laws of social development, on recognition of the dominant role of labour in human development, and on the teachings of the natural sciences and of socialist labour studies. The scientific organisation of work is based on the practical co-operation of workers, engineers and academic staff.

Table 1 lists the aims of the scientific organisation of work, the means employed in achieving it, the activities involved and the fields to which it applies.

The scientific organisation of work is designed to cover the study and improvement of—

(a) organisation at the work station;

(b) the supply and equipment of work stations;

(c) working methods and work processes;

(d) the division of labour, co-operation at work and the combination of operations in respect of the reciprocal adjustment of men and machines, the

Table 1. The scientific organisation of work: aims, means employed, activities involved and fields to which it applies

Aims	Means	Main activities involved	Planning and prepara- tion of production	Ongoing performance
			Particular fields to which organisation applies	
Improvement of conditions of work Development of personality Increase of labour productivity Cost reduction	Work study Job design Establishment of output norms Job classification Establishment of scales of remuneration	Organisational improvements at the workplace Improvement of tool and materials supply at the workplace Improvement of working methods and work processes Improvement of division of labour and co-operation within the plant Improvement of the system of output norms Improvement of conditions of work	Products Processes Investments Restructuring projects	Continuing improvement of processes already in use Main processes Setting up for production Management and administration

structure and distribution of tasks in the undertaking and the collective efforts of the workers;

(e) the system of remuneration and the material and moral rewards attached to the work done; and

(f) the physical conditions of work.

The means used are—

(a) work study;

(b) the issue of rules, guidelines and standards for work organisation models and the requirements to be met by the organisation of work; and

(c) job classification, comprising job evaluation and the establishment of wage scales.

Role of the authorities, of management and of the unions

Laws and regulations

In accordance with the Constitution, the Government has adopted legislation for the planned scientific organisation of work and for the protection of people in employment.

The Labour Code of 16 June 1977 defines the rights and obligations of undertakings and the role of trade unions with regard to the organisation of work (Chapter IV: Organisation of Work and Socialist Labour Discipline). The essential purposes of those provisions are, first, to facilitate increased production and the acceleration of scientific and technical progress, with a view to improving efficiency and the quality of work; and secondly to foster both personal development and the strengthening of the socialist way of life by regulating conditions of work in accordance with the most modern scientific knowledge. The Code also contains provisions to safeguard the citizens' constitutional right to health protection and maintenance of working capacity.

Under regulations of 17 April 1975 concerning the application of the system of scientific organisation of work, management is required to apply the results of labour studies when modifying work processes, when designing machinery, technological processes and plant, or when modernising existing undertakings or establishing new ones. The regulations lay down the basic rules governing work study, job design, job classification and output norms, as well as the guiding principles which undertakings must apply in order to improve the organisation of work, including above all the participation of the workers and the trade unions.

The Occupational Safety and Health Regulations of 14 December 1977 specify the obligations and duties of management in that respect under the Labour Code, and deal in particular with the action to be taken by managers of undertakings to make tools, machinery, equipment, work processes and workplaces safe and to eliminate abnormally trying conditions.

Under the regulations of 28 March 1973 concerning the tasks, rights and obligations of undertakings, combines and associations of public undertakings and amending regulations of 27 August 1973, managers must make use of the scientific organisation of work to ensure a steady rise in productivity and thus a limitation in the number of workers employed, as well as to increase the continuity of production and improve conditions of work. They must ensure that work processes are designed to permit high performance and to promote the development of the workers.

Besides this basic legislation, the Government has adopted provisions on particular subjects, such as the application of labour studies to product evaluation, investment decisions and the planning of work organisation.

In accordance with democratic principles, laws and regulations affecting the workers must be drawn up in conjunction with the unions and subject to their express agreement.

Research and scientific support

To provide a solid scientific foundation for the organisation of work and to assist management, the Government has set up research institutes such as the Central Labour Research Institute, the Central Occupational Safety and Health Institute and the Central Institute of Occupational Medicine. Over 40 institutions attached to technical training establishments, institutions of higher learning or government departments in charge of particular industries also engage in research work.

In most of the government departments in question there is a labour studies centre, which is associated with decision-making concerning the application of the knowledge acquired through labour studies and of the principles established on that basis. It advises management on the measures to be taken and provides direct assistance to individual undertakings. It lays down general guidelines for its own industry, co-ordinates labour studies within the department's field, undertakes special assignments on instructions from the Minister and deals with questions connected with further education and training in labour matters.

The structure of the system of the scientific organisation of work is shown in figure 1.

Responsibilities of management

The general managers of undertakings or the works managers are responsible for applying the system of scientific organisation of work, on the basis of the undertaking's own plan and the corresponding resources of the undertaking.

Role of the trade unions

As representatives of the workers' interests, the trade unions play an important part in the organisation of work. On the basis of their constitutional rights the unions have sponsored legislation, for example when the Labour Code was drawn up and discussed; they have also played a part in the adoption of other provisions, and have concluded agreements with state organs and with the management of combines and undertakings. With a view to ensuring the representation of the workers' interests and their active co-operation in the organisation of work, the presidium of the federal executive of the Confederation of Free German Trade Unions adopted on 27 June 1975 a resolution concerning the responsibilities and tasks of trade union committees and executives in respect of the heightening of the creative participation of the workers in the organisation of work. The resolution calls for—

(a) promoting the readiness of the workers to co-operate in work teams and restructuring and work organisation groups (see figure 1), and in socialist emulation, with a view to the scientific organisation of work;

(b) promoting the co-operation of public and trade union leaders with a view to ensuring the participation of the workers in the scientific organisation of work;

(c) organising co-operation between trade union committees and meetings of workers within the undertaking; and

(d) publicising the experience acquired by the best workers in applying the system of the scientific organisation of work and in respect of further training.

The resolution lays particular stress on trade union participation in the planning and direction of the organisation of work. This emphasis is reflected in works agreements. In connection with the restructuring of work, management and trade union leaders within the undertaking are to establish safe conditions of work that will be conducive to high performance; trying conditions are to be eliminated, hard manual work is to be reduced and occupational safety and health are to be improved. The unions exercise their rights of participation and supervision in all activities connected with the restructuring of work. Trade union organs within the undertaking express opinions and put forward proposals

Figure 1. Structure of the scientific system of work organisation (WO)

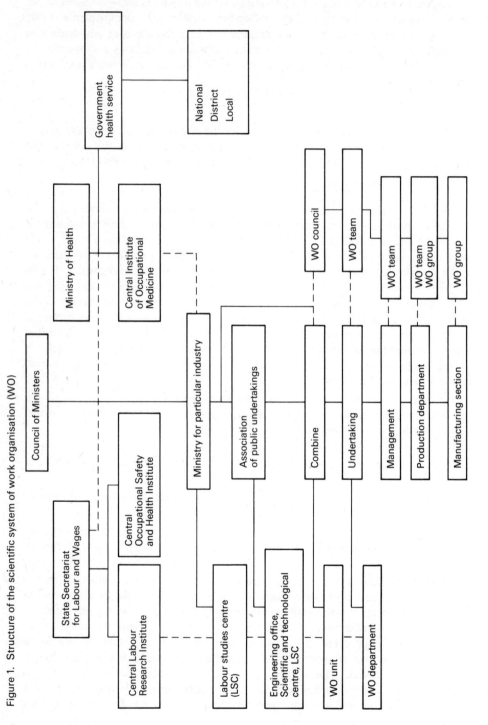

concerning decisions to be taken by the management. They assess the effects of investment policy and restructuring measures on conditions of work, keep co-operation with the workers under review and check up on the effect given to their proposals.

The regional and district committees of the Confederation of Trade Unions are also expected to supervise and co-operate in the application of the system of scientific organisation of work. They submit proposals concerning measures to be included in economic plans to the regional or district councils, help the unions in major undertakings to discharge their duties, and endeavour to pass on to smaller undertakings the experience thus acquired. The central trade union committees see to it that the labour studies centres are in a position to give effective help to undertakings and combines for the organisation of work.

Education and training

The organisation of work in undertakings requires the services of well trained specialists in labour studies. In fact all concerned—workers, supervisors, technical and administrative staff, managers—must have a sound training in this respect. Accordingly a system of initial and further education and training in labour matters has been established in the German Democratic Republic.

Initial training

Initial training with regard to the organisation of work consists in the imparting of suitable knowledge as part of vocational training, basic instruction in institutions of technical or higher education and specialisation in labour studies within the same institutions.

Induction training in labour matters is included in the classes on the organisation of the undertaking that are provided for in the vocational training programme of 1 September 1977. Examples drawn from the operation of the undertaking itself enable the trainees to become acquainted with the problems and methods of work organisation.

Basic instruction is included in the curriculum for studies in economic and technical subjects in institutions of technical or higher education, as well as in training courses for supervisors. It covers the purpose and methods of labour studies and the joint use of different branches of learning, particularly with regard to the organisation of work. Students learn to discern labour problems, to analyse them and to cope with them with the assistance of specialists.

Specialisation in labour studies is intended for students who will subsequently be employed as specialists in labour matters. In their final year these students can do work at a more advanced level on the labour side of some subject such as industrial engineering, economics, psychology, law or sociology.

Further training

Courses have been prepared to impart further training to workers and to technical and administrative staff in various institutions. Each syllabus covers the main subjects and the educational approach to be followed, and includes a bibliography and a list of teaching aids. While such a syllabus provides a uniform framework for the various training institutions, the adjustment of the training to each undertaking's particular needs is encouraged. The courses include a general course (of about 35 hours) on the scientific organisation of work and a course (of about 25 hours) on the principles of the scientific organisation of work in respect of the design of work stations; both of these courses are for skilled workers and supervisors. There are also other further training courses for technical and administrative staff.

For management staff further education courses in labour matters are organised by the Central Institute of Socialist Economic Management, the economic management institutes attached to certain institutions of higher learning and by the management schools for different sectors of the economy.

Various forms of further education in this field are also available for specialists in labour matters. Advanced courses on the labour side of industrial engineering and economics are run by institutions of higher and technical education. As a rule these courses take two years and combine direct and correspondence tuition. Another form of further training which also helps to build up the corps of supervisory, executive and technical staff is specialised training for skilled workers of proven capacity with regard to output norms. A compulsory syllabus on this subject has been drawn up by the state secretariats for labour and wages and for vocational training.

Various short courses on particular aspects of the organisation of work are also run by training bodies connected with undertakings, social organisations or the Government. Skeleton syllabuses are now being drawn up for such courses at the request of the State Secretariat for Labour and Wages.

All further education or training is voluntary. Nominations for participation in the courses are made by agreement between management and workers. In accordance with the socialist principles governing training policy, the workers chosen follow the courses free of charge, and are accorded study leave with pay. Outstanding performance can qualify the worker for material rewards and public congratulations from the sponsoring undertaking.

The socialist engineers' organisation, the Chamber of Technology, plays an important role with regard to further education in labour matters. The specialised associations and scientific or technical societies affiliated to it themselves draw up programmes of training to meet special needs, and run suitable courses at their own expense and on their own responsibility. Such courses include one on labour studies for technologists and another to train people to carry out investigations concerning safety and health. These extensive training activities have contributed to the widespread application of the system of scientific organisation of work in undertakings of the German Democratic Republic.

Results achieved

The use of the knowledge acquired through labour studies to promote a continuing improvement in the organisation of work has been fruitful: trying conditions and monotonous or tiresome tasks are being eliminated at an accelerating pace and there has been a qualitative change in the design of workplaces and work processes.

In accordance with government policy, an endeavour has been made since the beginning of the 1970s to assess the results achieved and to apply on a national scale the methods that have stood the test of time. Since 1973, work organisation measures have been included in the plans of undertakings. This has speeded things up and increased the influence exerted by the Government on the redesign of workplaces and the application of scientific knowledge to the design of new machinery and plant. Results show that these efforts have been successful. The number of work stations redesigned in accordance with the principles of labour studies rose from 28,000 in 1973 to 152,000 in 1975 and 219,000 in 1977. From 1974 to 1977 the number of persons called upon to work in trying conditions fell by 5 to 7 per cent each year; the decline amounted to 11.6 per cent in 1976 and 1977. About 67,000 workers thus benefited from improved conditions of work and better health protection. The scientific organisation of work also helped to reduce the number of cases of occupational accidents and diseases: from 1970 to 1976 the occupational accident rate fell by about 20 per cent, and the total number of man-days lost owing to occupational accidents and diseases by 19 per cent.

Over the past few years workers have co-operated extensively in the organisation of work. It is noteworthy that under the work restructuring programme the system of scientific organisation of work is applied by the workers themselves. The results achieved are largely due to improved design of work stations and to better supply arrangements and working methods (in manual work). These are fields in which the workers have much practical experience. Work organisation groups play an important role. They may or may not be permanent, and membership does not qualify for an increase in pay. Over 20,000 such groups, comprising 250,000 people, over half of them manual workers, are active in undertakings, combines and various institutions. With their assistance, over 50,000 work organisation measures, affecting over 170,000 jobs and 310,000 workers, were taken in 1976. The number of workers covered by such measures increases year by year.

APPLICATIONS

Restructuring of undertakings and work processes

General principles

The management of every undertaking in the German Democratic Republic is expected to restructure the production process in accordance with socialist principles. The overriding rule is that national economic performance must be improved not by exploiting the workers' capacity and injuring their health but by applying scientific knowledge to the work process. Managers must ensure that as efficiency increases the conditions in which work is performed are improved and its content is enriched. Specialists in labour matters lend assistance by trying out new measures and methods with management and by endeavouring to work out systems of general application.

Procedure

The procedure generally followed in restructuring is described below.

1. A restructuring project is worked out on the basis of—
   (a) the undertaking's output targets;
   (b) studies of production flow, the organisation of work, the technology used, the utilisation and efficiency of the workforce (with special reference to the workers' skills and conditions of work); and
   (c) the financial results of the unit concerned (section, department, undertaking as a whole).
2. Other studies are carried out as required, with the help of work study methods (general analyses and detailed studies of particular problems at the workplace).
3. Restructuring measures are worked out and decisions prepared for their implementation, in co-operation with the workers in the unit concerned.
4. Workplaces and processes are redesigned in accordance with the most advanced knowledge and with the experience the workers have acquired.
5. Output norms and performance indices are prepared and introduced, jobs are evaluated on the basis of a job classification, and remuneration (wages, bonuses and other benefits) is reviewed and amended in co-operation with the workers and by agreement with the unions.
6. The results of restructuring measures are evaluated with respect to their effects on conditions of work, productivity and costs.

Job enrichment

Assembly work is one of the major fields of application of the knowledge acquired through labour studies. Recommendations for fostering personal fulfilment on the workers' part have been drawn up to govern job design in electrical engineering and the electronics industry. Job design must serve three major purposes: it must guarantee the workers' safety and protect their health; utilise and develop their abilities, knowledge, qualifications and experience; and allow a high rate of productivity to be achieved. Steps are taken to ensure the greatest possible personal fulfilment, and attention is devoted to ascertaining what personality changes may be conducive to the attainment of that purpose.

Job enrichment covers all the job's requirements, be they physical (motor), psychological (sensory, intellectual, concentration) or personal (interests, attitudes, aspirations). The requirements are assessed by special methods applicable to the whole of industry; this ensures that the same principles are applied and the same measures taken throughout the country. If a job is to be well done, the job requirements and the workers' abilities must be closely matched. Wherever necessary, jobs are designed in such a way as to enable the workers to acquire additional knowledge and improve their qualifications, and to meet the job requirements after a specified time if they cannot do so at once. Job design thus ensures that the workers' abilities will be developed, and avoids assignment to jobs that do not give the workers enough scope. Four job enrichment methods that are used either on their own or in combination, as shown in figure 2, are described in the following pages.

Mechanisation and automation

To avoid under-utilisation of the workers' capacities, an attempt is made, in the first place, to eliminate boring, repetitive tasks through mechanisation or automation. The scope for such action must be considered at a very early stage, when production processes are selected. One has to see whether the particular process under consideration can be mechanised or automated at all, whether the process can be broken down into a co-ordinated sequence of operations and whether the workpiece can be handled by mechanised or automated installations. Care is taken to ensure that instead of itself giving rise to boring tasks, mechanisation or automation brings about a division of labour between man and machine that is conducive to job enrichment. The worker must not be left with purely residual functions consisting of the non-mechanised remainders of the original process; on the contrary, the worker must play an active operational role. It is easier to meet this requirement if mechanisation or automation is introduced in long sequences of operations, and if it gives rise to much more complex, qualitatively different tasks connected with the running or maintenance of the equipment.

Merger of operations

When production cannot be mechanised or automated, an attempt is made to ensure job enrichment by merging operations, especially those that have to be performed on each workpiece and that account for part of the operational time. The requirements of a job are largely determined by such operations, which being the most frequent may be said to constitute the core of the job. A merger of a series of operations with complementary requirements produces a job that promotes self-fulfilment.

The optimum duration of operational or cycle time varies according to the type of production and the conditions in the particular undertaking concerned. When cycle time does not exceed one minute it is very difficult to structure the tasks in such a way as to ensure personal fulfilment. Operations calling for concentration and thought must be substituted for those that are largely automatic once the worker has been trained to perform them. The worker must be given opportunities to take decisions and assume responsibility.

The operations that are merged may or may not have followed each other in a predetermined sequence as part of the technological process. The technical design of the product must be conducive to a division of labour; similarly, the method of manufacture of assemblies and sub-assemblies must be such as to provide maximum scope for the division of labour and for a form of job design that will promote personal fulfilment.

Besides the operations that are part of the regular job cycle and are repeated on each workpiece, due attention must also be paid to auxiliary operations, be they preparatory, accessory, or of a maintenance nature. In many cases (subject to technical and organisational limitations) job content can be enriched by

Figure 2. Examples of the scope of job enrichment in the German Democratic Republic

Methods	Enterprises			
	Kombinat VEB Pentacon, Dresden	VEB Robotron Elektronik, Radeberg	VEB Elektro-schaltgeräte, Dresden	VEB Messgeräte-werk, Beierfeld
Mechanisation and automation	X	X	X	X
Merger of operations:				
Merger of different operations falling in operational time	X	X	X	X
Merger of auxiliary and maintenance operations with production work in the narrow sense	X	—	—	X
Job rotation	—	X	—	X
Team work	—	—	—	X

associating some of these tasks with production work in the narrow sense. This method allows more varied job content, achieved for example through changes of posture or position or through changes in the nature of the intellectual effort or attention required. Auxiliary tasks also often provide more scope than directly productive tasks for communication within a work team. A merger of the two kinds of tasks, which are connected though not calling for performance in a predetermined sequence, increases the workers' autonomy and scope for decision-making. A job then entails an alternation of different requirements, which makes the work more meaningful and affords a wider range of creative opportunities.

Job rotation

The scope for improving job content is restricted by the technical requirements at particular work stations: the amount of equipment and the number of components that can be made available at a particular work station are often restricted by the nature and dimensions of the articles in question. Hence operations to be merged may in some cases have to be performed at different work stations, between which the workers must change over. Two cases can arise. The more common situation is one in which several workers are engaged in some operation and exchange work stations (where tasks differ from one work station to another). Job rotation can then either be scheduled or take place by agreement among the workers concerned. In the other case only one worker is required to perform the tasks performed at several work stations. In that case there is a change of work station, but not an exchange with another worker.

Job rotation allows a merger of a number of functions any one of which on its own would not be sufficiently rewarding for the worker in terms of personal fulfilment. Changes of work station must be sufficiently frequent to reduce the monotony of the various tasks, but not so frequent as to reduce performance. The worker must have at least two or three kinds of work or parts of an operation to perform consecutively in the course of the day or week. Finally it needs to be pointed out that the great advantage of this system is that it enables the workers to become multi-skilled.

Team work

Job rotation is a feature of team work, under which a team of workers is called upon to perform a complex assignment consisting of a series of different elements. The teams comprise between four and eight workers, who can perform all the operations involved and who move from one work station to another. The team is responsible for the entire assignment, including quality control. Conditions are the same for all its members, with regard, for example, to performance indices, wage scales and methods of payment.

The content of a team's collective assignments is determined by technological requirements. Tasks are organised in such a way that cycle time will not exceed about 30 minutes. Three cases can arise. In the first, the team's assignment comprises a series of phases, with an equal number of work stations and workers for each. In the second, there are numerous phases and a corresponding number of work stations but a lower number of workers (in order to ensure balanced use of capacity), so that the workers must change work stations individually in addition to the formal job rotation within the team. In the third case the number of phases is smaller than the number of workers and work stations, so that some tasks are performed simultaneously at several work stations and no job enrichment would be achieved by moving from one of these work stations to another.

By increasing the adaptability of the workforce, team work facilitates rapid adjustment to new conditions as time goes by. In terms of personal development team work for the execution of a complex assignment is very rewarding, since the workers are called upon to play an active part and to remain constantly in touch with their workmates: this kind of work helps to develop a sense of responsibility and to improve social behaviour. Team work has been found to bring about more co-operation, greater job satisfaction, an improvement in the quality of the work and a marked rise in productivity. An example is the introduction of team work for the assembly of electrical temperature transducers at the Beierfeld measuring equipment factory. The team consists of five women workers, and assembly comprises 12 operations, all of which can be performed by any of the workers in the team. The sequence of operations and the layout of work stations are shown in figure 3. An efficient layout has been introduced even though the process has to be carried out in a rather old building. The five workers, previously employed on an assembly line, carry out all the assembly work, from start to finish, moving from one work station to another under a rotation system which they organise themselves. They have a degree of autonomy and quite a wide range of activities; these factors, in conjunction with the possibility of moving from one kind of task to another, makes the work more interesting, promotes keenness and increases job satisfaction.

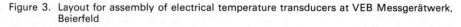

Figure 3. Layout for assembly of electrical temperature transducers at VEB Messgerätwerk, Beierfeld

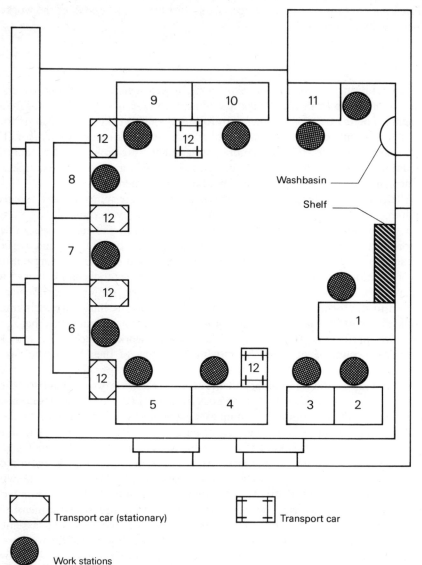

1. Riveting of the protective sheath
2. Soldering of the resistance
3. Soldering of the rivet on the top of the resistance
4. Lettering
5. Insertion of the elements in the sheath
6. Preliminary checking
7. Closing of the sheath
8. Final checking
9. Cleaning
10. Packaging
11. Repair
12. Placing on cars

Work organisation models

In 1972 or thereabouts, on the basis of experience acquired in the USSR and in other socialist countries, work organisation models began to be prepared for the most common types of employment, and binding methodological principles were laid down on the basis of the scientific design of plant and production processes. In that connection increasing use is being made of lists of requirements, job descriptions, indices of the standard of work organisation and evaluation guidelines.

The models are based on labour studies and economic objectives, and include design rules for a category of jobs. The basic idea is to arrive at a uniform model for a group of kindred tasks, with due attention to human fulfilment at work and higher productivity. The decisive advantage of this arrangement is that it can be applied to entire series of cases. A high standard of organisation of work can be achieved throughout the economy, especially for very common occupations and for jobs in which particularly expensive equipment is required. The work involved in designing restructuring projects is also considerably reduced by this means. The models cover—

(a) definition of the scope of each scheme;

(b) equipment and physical layout of work stations;

(c) characteristics of the workpiece;

(d) specifications for supply and despatching arrangements;

(e) sequence of operations, financial and performance indices, quality standards;

(f) workers' qualifications and responsibilities;

(g) the aesthetic side of industrial design; and

(h) occupational health and safety, including fire protection.

The elaboration and application of work organisation models is covered by government recommendations and rules and is part of the planning process. To ensure uniformity of approach, methodological guidelines have been drawn up for the use of government departments. There is a compulsory national standard on the subject for the economy as a whole. The elaboration of the models takes place in the following stages:

(a) identification of the workplaces or sectors of production for which models are needed;

(b) study of the workplaces or sectors in question;

(c) determination of the requirements to be met for the workplaces or sectors in question, on the basis of knowledge derived from labour studies and due allowance being made for technical limitations and economic objectives;

(d) study of design variations in the light of the various factors that must be allowed for in the model;

(e) elaboration of a proposed model (i.e. selection of the most advantageous possibility in respect of each factor);

(f) pilot run;

(g) final adjustments; and

(h) formal adoption.

The models form a uniform series of documents made available through a central information service. This system ensures that they will be quickly and extensively applied. About 160 models had been drawn up in the German Democratic Republic by the time of writing.

In light industry nine such models have allowed the redesign of work stations for machine work, as well as a considerable improvement in the working conditions of 20,000 workers. In building and public works the Dresden VEB Betonleichtbaukombinat had drawn up a work organisation model for the straightening and cutting of steel reinforcements. Besides a marked improvement in health and safety, there was a productivity increase of about 70 per cent; technical measures and the new form of work organisation enabled idle time to be reduced and several machines to be run by a single worker. On the occasion of the design of a new technological process, 13 work organisation models were established for the production, transport and assembly of sanitary facilities. In mechanical engineering the development of new machine tool models is continually accompanied by the preparation of corresponding models of work organisation: nine new work organisation models for typical jobs were prepared and tried out in 1977. The documents on the subject are available to all the government departments concerned with mechanical engineering.

Work organisation models are only one means of improving the design of workplaces and work processes. Other means of dealing with special problems that arise in particular industries are also being developed: for example there are design handbooks for work stations in the metal trades and for women, and catalogues of standardised equipment and of efficiency devices.

For the purposes of job design and the elaboration of work organisation models, undertakings, combines and research units have prepared job description cards, which are punched cards containing information on the essential features of the job, its economic, technological and organisational aspects, the job content, health and safety hazards and the organisation of work. The systematic introduction of such cards, which is now being planned, will be very useful for the design of workplaces and conditions of work, for the study of workload and the filling of posts with a view to the optimum utilisation of labour, for occupational health services and for the improvement of conditions of work and of production at the level of the undertaking. The system allows a job card index to be built up in each undertaking and used for a variety of purposes by all departments; it is the first step towards the constitution of such indexes for entire sectors of the economy. In the chemical industry these cards must already be used for any job analysis. An initial survey provided data on the 16,000 jobs of over 50,000 production workers. A comprehensive survey to provide data for centralised analysis on 300,000 workers in the industry is to be completed by 1980.

Organisational indices

The systematic application of the knowledge acquired through labour studies is not entirely a matter for specialists. Managers of undertakings and combines must ensure that it does not become so, by taking appropriate action in agreement with trade union leaders. To facilitate such action, it was necessary to find some practical means of ascertaining as accurately as possible, in numerical terms, the standard of work organisation reached, and subsequently, on the same basis, to specify the progress to be made and monitor the attainment of the targets. Prompted by the experience acquired in undertakings in the USSR, a system was worked out by the Central Labour Research Institute, the Central Institute of Occupational Medicine and the Central Institute of Occupational Health and Safety. It is already applied in undertakings, where it has been found to be a useful management tool. It consists of ten indices of the standard of work organisation reached.

The value of the indices ranges from 0 to 1 (1 being always the standard to be attained). They can be used separately or in conjunction, and measure the following factors:

(a) preparation and application of labour-saving measures (time saving);

(b) production flow;

(c) utilisation of machinery and plant (in relation to the available capacity and the possible duration of utilisation);

(d) utilisation of working time;

(e) achievement of quality standards;

(f) stability of employment of supervisory, executive and technical staff;

(g) proportion of accepted orders actually filled;

(h) good housekeeping;

(i) safety (technical prevention); and

(j) occupational health.

The definitions are partly verbal and partly mathematical. The good house-keeping index, for example, is an average of indices of tidiness and cleanliness of the workplace, care of machinery, tools and equipment, and state of the sanitary and welfare facilities. The index of occupational health covers ten factors, including microclimate, dust, noise, vibrations, lighting, exposure to harmful chemicals, danger of infection and difficulty of the work. The hazards are assessed in terms of intensity and duration of exposure, according to a scale which is reproduced below in a simplified form:

Index	*Description*
1.0	No exposure, no health impairment.
0.8	Exposure without health impairment (maximum permissible limits not exceeded).
0.5	Low probability of health impairment (exposure to the maximum permissible limits).
0	Serious health hazard (maximum limits constantly exceeded by a substantial margin).

The application of the system of indices of the standard of work organisation calls for advanced labour studies and well organised participation by different sections of the undertaking. The data required are collected and the indices compiled by the work study department, the management and the workers in the departments concerned with production proper, the preparation of production and accounting. The work study department must analyse and utilise the indices as a basis for action to be taken by the various production departments. The indices have already been successfully used in undertakings and for certain sectors of the economy. In the brown coal industry, for example, improvements in working conditions based on the use of the indices were introduced for 2,200 workers in 1972, 9,275 in 1973 and 13,000 in 1974.

Equipment and process development

The socialist organisation of production ensures that technology serves human ends, and develops in accordance with human abilities and requirements. The Government's economic policy calls on management to eliminate trying or dangerous conditions, and to organise the work in such a way as to protect the workers' health and increase efficiency. Provisions are laid down for safety and health inspection in undertakings and for the improvement of occupational medicine and welfare services in the workers' interests. These objectives must be borne in mind in particular when production facilities are being modernised or new establishments set up, as well as in the design of new or improved machines, processes and equipment. In that respect labour studies play a major role in addition to technology. The results to be achieved through labour studies depend on their application to the production process. Labour studies can be most extensively and profitably applied to the preparation of production—i.e. in all research, development and design work and in the establishment and implementation of investment policy. In the various aspects of the preparation of production, particular attention is devoted to ensuring that technical and economic objectives are considered in conjunction with the objectives of labour studies, in order to make work easier and more interesting, to promote human well-being at work and, simultaneously, to make the best use of technology, eliminate waste, ensure continuous production and ensure widespread application of the best working methods and of the lessons to be drawn from the workers' experience.

Knowledge derived from labour studies is being applied in the following fields:

(a) in the setting up of new production plants or the modernisation of plants already in existence;

(b) in research and development concerning products and processes, and incorporation of the results in production (fixing of targets, adjustments, evaluation);

(c) in facilitation of research and technical development, and in the preparation of various aids for specialists—engineers, technologists, economists—of the production preparation staff (including in particular the lists of job requirements and the work organisation models); and

(d) in the continuing development of initial and further education and training in labour matters (especially for research and development staff) and in the strengthening of socialist co-operation between specialists (engineers or technicians) and the workers who are called upon to erect and operate new plants.

Two examples

Design and construction of agricultural machinery

The guiding consideration in equipment and process development is that job classification and the kind of work process will be determined by the design of plant and equipment in accordance with the lessons derived from labour studies. The application of this principle is illustrated by the development of a new series of agricultural machines. These machines—self-powered combine harvesters—were designed and introduced side by side with the development of industrial production methods in socialist agriculture. The characteristics of the new machines were determined on the basis of the scientific organisation of operations and the development of working methods in agriculture, and the results of labour studies were also taken into account. The design and development work was governed by the guidelines for project preparation, in the light of national economic targets and of forecasts and results derived from pure and applied research, as well as by more detailed provisions concerning the development of products, processes and plant. In accordance with the lists of requirements, the corresponding guidelines, work organisation models and so forth, labour studies were carried out at various stages of the development of these machines in accordance with the plan of the undertaking. The results were to be assessed and formally adopted in accordance with the laws and regulations.

The results of this procedure can be assessed in terms of the performance of the machines developed and introduced in agriculture (see table 2). Model E 175 is the first combine harvester produced in the German Democratic Republic; the more recent models E 512 and E 516 are those now in use.

These results could not have been achieved without a steady improvement in conditions of work and changes in work content. In close co-operation with research bodies, the "Fortschritt" combine developed a large number of valuable improvements. Improved cab design led to a marked reduction in such objectionable features of the work as dust, exposure to toxic chemicals, noise and vibration. Intelligent machine design and improved controls, in particular, made the work much easier, both physical and mental effort being reduced and operating comfort improved. Experience fully confirmed the value of the general procedure followed in work study units at the level of the undertaking with regard to the application of the results of labour studies. To facilitate the task of designers and technologists, research bodies prepared numerous new tools, including a compendium of labour study guidelines. These guidelines focus upon programme sequences or flow charts which are used in production preparation. They are supplemented by tables, summaries and illustrations, so that there is no need to refer to any other source of information. The use of the compendium of

Table 2. Comparative efficiency of three models of combine harvester
(E 175 = 100)

Criterion	Model	
	E 512	E 516
Area harvested	250	500
Cost of harvesting per hectare	70	65
Labour required per hectare	40	20

labour study guidelines has had a very favourable effect on all that pertains to the preparation of production.

Restructuring in the mechanical engineering industry

The modernisation of undertakings, the introduction of new processes and equipment, the erection of new plants and the establishment of new undertakings in key sectors of the economy are all proceeding apace in the German Democratic Republic. The example of the Hartha works producing telescopic shock absorbers for the automobile industry illustrates the application of labour studies by showing how a modernisation project is worked out and implemented and how the system of scientific organisation of work is applied.

The project was designed and implemented on the basis of a flow chart (figure 4) governing the application of the nine stages of the project to the product, the plant, the production processes and the work involved. The first four stages are of particular importance, since it is at those stages that basic decisions are taken concerning conditions of work, environmental design, the organisation of work and work content.

From the point of view of labour studies, the problem at the Hartha works was above all to ensure maximum utilisation of the existing and potential capacity of the workforce. An endeavour was made to enrich job content by changing the division of labour and work co-operation arrangements, by introducing new methods and by improving the equipment of work stations. The project also provided for the restructuring and mechanisation of auxiliary operations, especially maintenance, transport and stock management, with a view to reducing unhealthy, arduous and boring work to a minimum. To encourage co-operation and mutual assistance among the workers, attention had to be devoted to the possibilities of improving information media and means of communication, and of improving the composition of work groups. All technical and organisational measures had to meet occupational safety and health requirements.

For the purposes of project design and implementation, the central research bodies and the research units of government departments and of the health service made available much methodological material, which is being put to increasing use and steadily improved. The material includes model schemes of work organisation, job descriptions, product descriptions, lists of requirements to be met at workplaces and in production operations, work design guides for particular trades or undertakings, and codes of safe operating practice for

Figure 4. Flow chart for the application of labour studies (LS) to the consideration and design or re-structuring projects

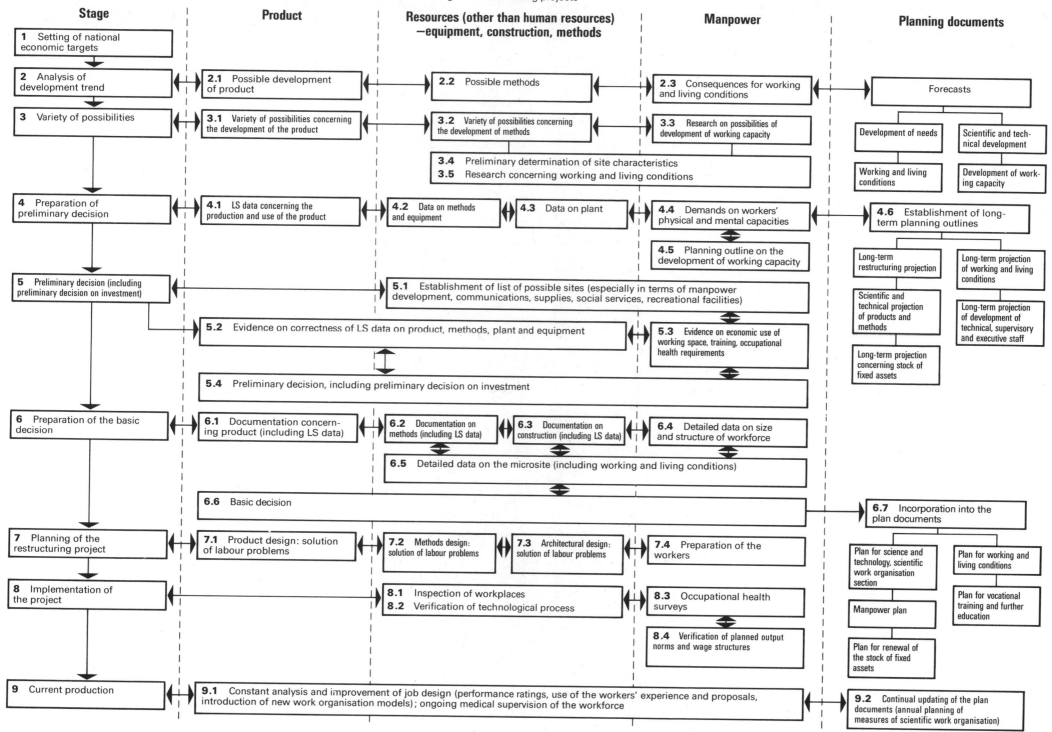

particular trades. The implementation of the project, the speedy application of the decisions taken to the production process and their subsequent amendment all rest on the regular comparison of set targets and results achieved, with the help, in particular, of indices of the standard of work organisation. Steps are taken to ensure that conditions are in every respect satisfactory at every stage.

The complex work carried out in this undertaking, together with the assistance of scientific bodies which enabled the knowledge acquired in the field of labour studies to be applied to the solution of technical and economic problems, produced quite a number of results, the principal ones being as follows. Difficult, arduous or dangerous work was eliminated. Jobs specially adapted to feminine physical and physiological requirements, and calling for a higher degree of skill, were designed for women. For some operational work (tempering, painting, assembly and stock management) the division of labour was reconsidered when mechanisation was introduced, so that job content was enlarged and the work made more responsible. Mechanisation and automation were accompanied by the introduction of new forms of work organisation which promote self-fulfilment, encourage co-operation and increase productivity. All these measures have increased the workers' satisfaction and pride in their undertaking.

The systematic application of the results of labour studies in restructuring projects also entails co-operation with official local bodies. In the case of the Hartha works this involved arrangements concerning facilities for shift workers, medical supervision, the organisation of transport to and from the works for the staff and improvement of child-care facilities. Although such measures may not be part of the organisation of work, it is undoubtedly much affected by them.

INDIA

INDIA
Nitish R. De*

NATIONAL CONDITIONS

It is not very widely known that while research on new forms of work organisation was in progress in the British coal industry, a similar experiment was started in a cotton textile manufacturing group in Ahmedabad in 1953.[1] The new "whole-task" approach was introduced into four loom sheds, two automatic and two non-automatic, in the Calico Mills and the Jubilee Mills. Results of the experiment were reported in terms of productivity as well as worker involvement. The evaluation revealed that the "whole-task" approach to formation of the work group, a basic tenet of the socio-technical approach to organisation of work, resulted in substantially increased earnings for the workers. Although the cost of production was somewhat higher, this was more than compensated for by higher output; more significantly, product damage was 59 per cent lower than it had been before.

A follow-up study carried out in 1970[2] indicated that only in one of the four workplaces where the group system of work had been introduced—a non-automatic loom shed—had work organisation and levels of performance remained unchanged over the intervening 16 years. In the other loom sheds the new work systems had been abandoned. The evaluation indicates that the setback was partly caused by inability to keep the new work forms attuned to changing technology and to customers' product tastes.

One issue that inevitably arises out of such mixed results is that of cultural relevance and relativity.[3] Indian workers are not accustomed to participating in the decision-making process, whether in the arena of politics, in the work situation, or in trade union activities;[4] they tend to feel that decision-making is rightly centralised in the hands of the managerial group. One reason adduced is that workers are disqualified from decision-making by their lack of education. Indian workers are thought to be more interested in job security, redressal of individual grievances at work, and good pay and working conditions. Indian managers, on the other hand, attach the highest importance to their own security and esteem needs and the least importance to their own need for self-

---

* National Labour Institute, New Delhi.

actualisation.[5] They are very sensitive about status; they profess belief in group-based participative decision-making but have little faith in the capacity of their subordinates for taking initiative and responsibility; and they are convinced that managers have to compromise ethics and morals in order to accomplish what they may be thought to regard as a manipulative task. On the whole, they are authority-conscious in the sense of being reluctant to share power.

The Ahmedabad experiment did not spread throughout the Sarabhai group of companies where it started in the two cotton textile mills, nor did it evoke much interest in other Indian industries. However, in 1973 a workshop was organised in Calcutta and attended by senior managers and trade union leaders from some of the major public enterprises and one government department. The results were favourable and at least two organisations showed interest in undertaking pilot projects on work redesign as a way of overcoming employee apathy to work.

In July 1974 the National Labour Institute was set up as an autonomous body in New Delhi, and gave high priority to industrial democracy. A series of workshops was planned from October 1974, and in the course of two years 23 seminars, workshops and programmes were organised in different parts of the country. Over 1,150 government administrators, industrial managers and trade union leaders attended.

These activities were meant to develop discussion concerning current conditions of work and life of wage earners and salaried employees, young managers and people at higher echelons, in the context of the prevalent technology and employee motivation. Carefully selected cases from other countries were presented for group examination and discussion. Initially, top managers from industry were invited to participate in these meetings. Their response was understandably mixed, ranging from guarded to open. Simultaneously, trade union leaders were invited. These early efforts and group discussions led to specific invitations from some of the major industrial and government organisations to start action-research projects on industrial democracy in early 1975. Thus the seed that had been sown in December 1973 started taking roots in early 1975, in large measure through the efforts of the National Labour Institute.

CASE STUDIES

Bharat Heavy Electricals Ltd.

Bharat Heavy Electricals is one of the largest public enterprises in India, with four major manufacturing plants in existence and two under construction. Some of the existing plants such as those at Tiruchirapalli and Hyderabad have been undergoing expansion with a view to covering a wider range of products. The enterprise employs over 56,000 people in manufacturing, marketing, research and development, servicing and corporate management. Some of the output is exported. The corporation has made singular progress since 1972, and experiments with new forms of work organisation have met with a considerable degree of success in the enterprise's works at Hardwar, where the Ganges emerges from the foothills of the Himalayas, and at Tiruchirapalli, some 320 km south-west of Madras, as well as in the central foundry forge located near the Hardwar works.

Hardwar

The Hardwar unit, which employs over 9,000 people, is mainly engaged in the manufacture of heavy electrical equipment such as steam and hydraulic turbines, generators and related equipment. Advice has been provided under a technical collaboration agreement by a large Soviet undertaking located in Leningrad. The design and manufacturing activities have been taken over gradually by the Indian counterparts as they have gathered experience and confidence. However, although the unit had been in existence for over ten years, its productivity was by no means satisfactory.

Having attended a quality of working life seminar, the executive director of the unit became interested in having action along those lines initiated in the plant. By request, a National Labour Institute team of consultants started discussions with the managers, the trade union leaders (there were four identifiable trade unions in operation) and the supervisory staff. The discussions, held occasionally in separate groups and at times in joint sessions, gradually moved all concerned towards a resolution that a pilot project should be started at a favourable work-site.

It may also be mentioned here that a comprehensive survey was undertaken in the unit to determine the training needs of supervisors[6] and another survey to explore the relationship between the perception of life at work and life in the community. The first survey revealed significant differences among individuals in terms of knowledge of such essential subjects as the unit's products, elementary engineering and the personnel practices of the organisation. Ignorance of these subjects was certainly not conducive to effective performance of supervisory functions. The second study, to establish relationships between the quality of family and community life and the quality of working life, was still in progress at the time of writing. Preliminary data[7] can be tentatively regarded as indicating that a clear cleavage exists between the life of the workers at the workplace and their life within the family. If anything, no positive aspect from one part of their lives has a spill-over effect on another. On the contrary, the workers' existence in those two separate worlds causes tension in family life. These findings further confirmed management and workmen in their desire to launch quickly a programme for combating the alienation arising from the work system itself.

Block V in the Hardwar plant, where 25 workmen were engaged in fabrication of the upper part of a condenser unit, was selected for the pilot experiment in view of its compact character, reasonable layout and the positive attitude of the manager and the shop-floor trade union leaders. There were other compelling reasons to choose this shop. The condenser in question is an expensive piece of equipment, costing over 12 million rupees. Secondly, for setting up a power station, it was necessary that a condenser unit should be placed at the site before the steam turbine was installed, and it was desirable that the condenser should be manufactured and despatched at least two months before the completed steam turbine. Thirdly, productivity in the shop was not high. The shop was thus an ideal spot for initiating improvement measures.

The workers covered by the pilot experiment participated in a series of meetings with both internal and external consultants, and agreed that the work should be redesigned. The total complement of 25 workers in Block V was made up of 9 fitters, 3 fettlers, 3 welders, 2 gas-cutters, 1 crane operator, 2 riggers, 2 helpers, and 3 workmen involved in materials supplies.

Discussions centred on a variety of work-flow analyses, including a study of the social system of work as imposed by the technology involved. This study indicated, first, that each worker was concerned exclusively with his own trade. None of them really identified himself with the product. Secondly, there was invariably forced idle time because when a particular worker was engaged at a given location, another who was required to work in close proximity had to wait until the first worker had finished his job. Thirdly, there was uneven demand on the services of the materials supplies group, the crane operator and the riggers. It will be seen from figure 1A that when the studies were undertaken in April and May 1975 productivity was certainly low. In the ensuing summer months the low level of productivity was partly due to high absenteeism.

When all the data, as generated by the workers from their own experiences, had been analysed, the workers decided on two steps. First, a task force should be set up comprising representatives of each category of workers together with the supervisor. While two of its members should be on it permanently because of their leadership abilities, the other members, except for the supervisor, should be appointed in rotation. The task force numbered eight. The manager under whom the shop was placed would also participate in meetings of the task force if it so wanted, and an industrial engineer was associated the task force as a consultant.

Secondly, it was decided that a new work system should be devised which would improve the workers' motivation as well as overcoming the persistently low productivity. After deliberations, the task force, with the concurrence of the employees concerned, evolved a work system in which the direct production group would consist of one welder, three fitters and one fettler. The group should take charge of the complete task, and its members would gradually take up one another's job by undergoing on-the-job training assisted by the supervisor, the industrial engineer and their fellow workers. Cross-skilling would also be introduced between the crane operator and the riggers. It was decided that the gas-cutters and helpers on the one hand and the materials supplies group on the other would be integrated into the new work system at a later stage. As the system came into operation a number of advantages and drawbacks emerged. On the positive side, a welder now started working as a fitter and if he did not know the art of reading elementary drawings, which was a necessity for a fitter's job, arrangements were made by the management to provide on-the-job training. Similarly, training in the other trades of their work groups was given to fitters, fettlers, gas-cutters and others.

With more experience and confidence, the workers co-operating with the task force brought about a second redesign of their work organisation in September

Figure 1. Efficiency in Blocks II, IV and V of the Hardwar unit of Bharat Heavy Electricals
Ltd., April 1975-October 1976

A. Blocks II and V (manufacture of condenser units)

Efficiency (per cent.)

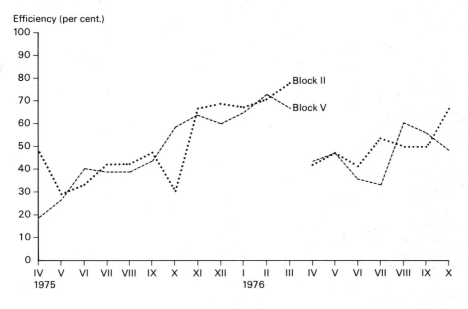

B. Block IV (closed panel assembly section)

Efficiency (per cent.)

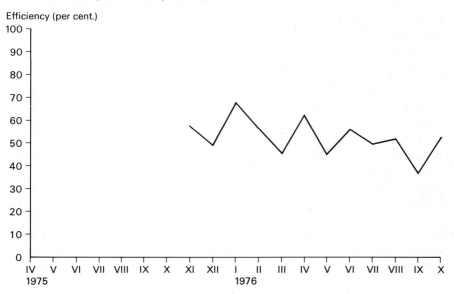

1975. It was decided that the workforce should be distributed in two shifts in the following manner:

Shift 1	*Shift 2*
Fitters 5	Fitters 4
Welders 5	Welders 4
Gas-cutter 1	Gas-cutter 1
Fettler 1	Fettler 1

In addition, there would be crane operators in both the shifts. Each shift group became integrated and self-contained. It was decided that one shift would fabricate the right side of the upper part of the condenser unit; the other shift would do the same with the left side. As and when a pair of sides were completed the two groups would then weld them together in order to complete the upper part of the condenser.

The new work system started in Block V late in May 1975. Block II, concerned with the manufacture of the lower part of the condenser unit, started applying the same system in June. The senior supervisor of the shop took the initiative and 39 workmen of similar trades as mentioned above were involved. Here also the task force consisted of eight members, with monthly rotation.

With the introduction of the new form of work organisation there was an improvement in productivity, although there were also occasional setbacks. Progressively the old pattern of one-man, one-function was superseded by the acquisition of multiple skills and the development of a group system of working, with internal monitoring of group norms, internal control of work flow and work allocation, and identification with the product and its quality. Particularly significant from the management's point of view was the gradual drop in personal idle time (e.g. time spent loitering about at the workplace, or spent outside the workplace without justifiable reasons). The commitment of the workers, the supervisor and the manager was distinctly apparent.

It is worth mentioning that the target of seven condensers for the year 1975-76 was completed as far as the workers of Block V were concerned by January 1976, with the result that the management had to give them other work from February 1976. The demand for thermal power sets for the year 1976-77 having declined, the need for condensers was also much reduced, and the workers in Blocks II and V therefore had to manufacture other products of which they had not had much experience. It is interesting to note that both groups responded positively to the challenge. The switch-over from the manufacture of condensers to other types of product indeed affected productivity adversely and caused initial disruption in group working. Significantly, however, the amount of tension between management and workers that could otherwise be generated in a similar situation was absent. They worked together to overcome the challenge, and by November 1976 there was no sign of tension at all due to the switch-over. Figure 1A indicates that with the new product mix productivity in these two shops was slowly and steadily rising.

It also seems that despite the new demands on the workers for involvement in new product lines, their urge to maintain multiple skills continued. In contrast to the usual union-management type of meeting in which interest-related issues dominate, the minutes of task force meetings indicate a high degree of orientation towards work-interest issues such as delay in the repair of a crane, the repair of welding sets, improving the system of on-the-job training, a joint search to identify the forces contributing to lower productivity and a search for ways to reduce job tension. In fact, an examination of the agenda papers and the minutes of meetings of the task forces of Blocks II and V from April 1975 to October 1976 reveals a distinct shift towards looking at a problem as a collective one instead of trying to make a scapegoat of the other party.

The possibilities of diffusion have been under active consideration by both the workers and the management, but the initiative in starting new projects in particular shops was left to the employees of the shops concerned. In September 1975 Block IV came forward, and through a series of meetings with the 20 workmen concerned it was decided to start the project in the closed panel assembly section. Eighteen workers were involved in the project, the key categories being fitters, electricians and machine operators. Here too, a task force was set up consisting of five persons, including the supervisor.

Two particular problems were highlighted during the experiment in Block IV. One was that after the closed panel assembly work had reached an advanced stage, a design change was often forced on the work group by technological necessity; almost complete reworking might be required. This was considered wasteful, since time was being lost; more than that, it caused the workers a great deal of frustration. When the group system was introduced the discontent among the workmen caused by last-minute design changes came to the forefront and the task force and the management jointly decided that close liaison with the design group should be maintained in order to eliminate such irritating practices, or at any rate reduce them to a minimum. With concerted efforts, improvements started taking place. The management also decided that time spent on rework on account of certain design changes should not affect the workers' bonus earnings.

The primary problem in Block IV, however, was that while it was comparatively easy for an electrician to learn to do the job of a fitter through in-service training, it was ultimately found that by such methods a fitter could not learn to do an electrician's job without committing errors beyond tolerance. The task force had become quite confident of success, and in September 1976 it had decided that there should be almost a complete switch-over of jobs between fitters and electricians. This move turned out to be premature: work efficiency fell to 37.5 per cent (as shown in figure 1B), bonus earnings were reduced, and this created a degree of tension. On reflection, the task force then decided in October 1976 to introduce a revised programme of training. It should be realised that the work in Block IV is considered somewhat more complicated than the work carried out in Blocks II and V.

Since September 1976 new forms of work organisation have also been introduced in Block I (turbo-rotor coil section and detailed assembly section) and Block III (rotor assembly production and blading section) and in the personnel department. In the latter department, consisting of 22 persons, there had been three divisions—one dealing with the plant operation and maintenance, another with design and commercial matters and the third with the policy matters located in the office of the executive director. The department reorganised itself into three operating groups—one dealing with all the problems of supervisory, clerical and ministerial staff, another with the skilled category of workers and the third with the semi-skilled and unskilled. The functional division of the department's work was thus eliminated, a three-man co-ordinating team being set up so to ensure that the three groups functioning autonomously would not come to contradictory conclusions and policy recommendations. According to the reports of the office assistants, who belong to the clerical category, this new system of work is much more satisfying than the fragmented type of work to which they had previously been accustomed.

The reorganisation of work led to enlargement of the supervisory role in the form of liaison between the input and output departments and service units, and involvement in central planning. This became possible because the work groups assumed substantial control over the production process, including routine inspection and maintenance activities, in addition to implementation of rules of discipline. All this experience encouraged the management and the task forces to set up separate project teams to deliberate on and submit reports on the following three themes:

(a) multi-skill training, its role in employee satisfaction and higher productivity; encouraging the motivating factors for workers to acquire skills in different trades;

(b) the changing role of supervisors, particularly in respect of co-ordination, planning and training; and

(c) diffusion of the scheme of work redesign to white-collar staff working in such areas as the personnel, finance and medical departments.

The project teams consisting of managers and the workers from three blocks where the work redesign experiments were conducted—Blocks II, IV and V—submitted their reports to the management, which examined them in consultation with the workmen concerned.

Central foundry forge plant

Construction of the central foundry forge plant, located near the Hardwar unit, began in October 1974. When operating at full capacity, it will employ 2,500 persons making heavy castings and forgings primarily for heavy electrical equipment.

Encouraged by the experiences of the Hardwar plant, the management took care to foster team work from the very beginning. Social distinctions between worker and worker and between worker and manager on the basis of differences in their respective knowledge and skills were discouraged. All employees, including engineers, were encouraged to become multi-skilled so as to avoid a rigid compartmentalisation of work. Contrary to the Indian industrial tradition, the management deliberately decided that all workers would be given the designation of "operative" instead of trade-based designations like "fitter", "machinist" and so on.

One consequence of the new system was that from the beginning morale was found to be high in the plant and construction bottlenecks were reduced to a minimum. As a result of a spirit of close co-operation at work, the 10-tonnes arc furnace was commissioned in April 1976, four months ahead of schedule and only 18 months after construction work had begun. Similarly, the 30-tonnes arc furnace was commissioned six months ahead of time, in November 1976. The machine shop was commissioned three months ahead of time and there were indications that the forge shop, the most expensive in the whole complex, would come into operation in June 1977 as against the target date of December 1977. The cast-iron foundry, which was handed over by the Hardwar unit to this plant, was initially producing 10 to 15 tonnes of finished product per month. With the same total complement of 162 employees, the plant was producing at the rate of 152 tonnes per month within one year. The "whole task" concept of work, applied both at the construction stage and the operation stage, is reflected throughout the plant. As one employee put it, every employee now looks upon himself as a "foundry man" rather than as one belonging to a particular designation or a particular trade. This has become the attitude as much of a fettler who also works as a heat treatment man as of a maintenance manager or a quality control manager who becomes involved in production work in the foundry shop or the forge shop whenever the need arises. The minutes of the shop council of the cast-iron foundry indicate that the six members (three representatives of the workers and three of the management) are very active in relation to work-related activities, interest-related activities remaining the legitimate function of traditional union-management relations.

Tiruchirapalli

Yet another significant case is that of the heavy boiler plant at Tiruchirapalli. Unlike the Hardwar plant, it operated from the very beginning with a high degree of efficiency and profitability. The plant was well known for its quality products, the progressive spirit of its management and its extremely good industrial relations climate. Action to improve the organisation of work was undertaken early in 1973 in two major work areas, the drum shop and the header shop. In the drum shop, although productivity was high, it was found that the cycle time of production could, on occasion, deviate from the norm by as much as eight weeks, whereas ideally it should not have been more than nine months plus or minus two weeks. It was felt that something had to be done to eliminate these excessive variations. The action taken, in consultation with the workers of the shop, focused on worker involvement in planning, decentralisation of decision-making, and improvement in product knowledge at all levels. Its highlights were as follows:

(1) A comprehensive welding plan for each month was prepared in consultation with the supervisors. It was prominently displayed in the shop and made available to each work team.

(2) The central lathe machine, the only such piece of equipment available in the shop, was normally available for use for no more than 40 or 45 hours a week.

This was considered a bottleneck, and after consultation between the workers and the consultant, a number of steps were taken. The shift arrangement was made flexible enough for the workers of the three shifts to decide the composition of personnel in each shift, including provision for switch-over should occasion demand it. Formerly, workers holding different trade designations had been concerned with different aspects of the operation of the machine. Under the new scheme the segmented work structure was abandoned and the whole team started working together; loading and unloading time were thus considerably reduced. Time lost on account of maintenance work was also reduced, by 10 per cent. The workers also designed certain jigs and fixtures to facilitate the operation of the machine. In addition, a lathe load chart indicating a weekly schedule for the entire month was prominently displayed for every worker to see. The records of daily shift performance in relation to the weekly target were also displayed.

(3) Similarly, in the electrode welding section, there was a need to reduce the rejection rate due to faulty welding. The personnel of the section as a whole diagnosed the problem and improved the method of working. The set target of a zero level of rejection was reached between November 1975 and May 1976.

(4) On account of their high level of specialisation the high-pressure welders, of whom there were 14 on each shift, could not be integrated in the newly constituted work teams, and they formed a specialised group on their own; it was autonomous in terms of daily allotment of tasks among members and co-ordination of activities between the shifts. This arrangement provided a degree of flexibility, so that depending on the pressure of work more welders could turn up on any particular shift.

In the header shop also, the new form of work organisation was introduced in August 1973, more or less at the same time as in the drum shop.

In each of the two shops there are five small groups. Every Saturday morning one representative of each group attended a meeting with the supervisor. The agenda covered a review of weekly performance, including analysis of shortfall or over-performance, quality improvement programmes, cost reduction, scheduling activity for the next week, the review of safety records and internal group norms. The planning process had thus become a grass-roots activity.

The results in the two production shops were regarded as encouraging, and work redesign systems were therefore also introduced, in August 1974, in the computer system section of the production engineering department. Evaluation of the system in May 1976 showed a higher degree of job satisfaction among employees at different levels, better service to the customers and closer adherence to the schedule for completion of projects, so that more computer time became available for developmental work.

Similarly, new forms of work organisation were introduced in the subdelivery section of the procurement department in 1974. This section is responsible for the purchase of materials amounting to some Rs. 200 million annually. Most of the subdelivery items require a long lead time for procurement since complexity of specifications often creates delays. Nearly half of these items are imported. Close examination revealed, not unexpectedly, that the executives in this section were continuously under heavy pressure of work, running behind time and suffering from high levels of anxiety. There was a felt need to change the strained work situation and to improve the work system in such a way that the delays could be avoided. The executives in the section created a work team to design alternative systems. From a bureaucratic assembly-line type of activity with papers and files moving up and down, a desk-oriented system was introduced utilising a job enrichment concept so that individual members of the staff could integrate different activities in their own roles. The control system has been decentralised, so that there is less pressure on the supervisory officials, more elbow room for executives dealing with an integrated range of purchase activities, a higher degree of job satisfaction reflected in a diminution of tension, bickering and evasion of responsibility, and a perceptible improvement in working relations between executives and their subordinates. Company directors have decided to extend the new forms of work organisation to other sections of materials management.

Government post office

In April 1975 the Director of Postal Training took the initiative in launching a work motivation research programme for employees in the post offices. He was generally encouraged by the senior officials in his efforts. During this time the Prime Minister of India was also showing her concern about the impression created on ordinary men and women by many subordinate government officials in day-to-day contact with the public. She mentioned, in particular, the behaviour, conduct and sensitivity of counter clerks in the post offices, bank employees, and employees in the hospitals as playing a key role in determining how a government was judged by the public.

A staff group of the National Labour Institute had a series of general discussions concerning work reorganisation with senior officials in the postal directorate, and then concerning more concrete details with the Postmaster-General at Ambala and the Senior Superintendent of Post Offices at Simla. On-the-spot studies were conducted, after which it was decided that Chaura Maidan post office at Simla would be an appropriate place to conduct an experiment. To evolve a new form of work organisation the internal and external consultants proposed a dialogue between the external consultants and the management, including the sub-postmaster who headed the organisation, and discussions between the management and all the employees of the post office.

The post office in question had 44 employees, 43 full time and one part time. There were union leaders working in this post office, two being postmen and one a telegrapher.

Information about job satisfaction that was obtained anonymously from the employees, particularly the postmen and clerks, showed that in the workers' perception the postal authorities' genuine interest in their welfare and job satisfaction was only average, their receptivity to the needs of the employees was low, and the effectiveness of the consultation before decisions were taken was also low. The majority of the employees felt that they had to do their particular work because they had no alternative means of earning a living. There was no real satisfaction with work content or the work climate.

The main tasks of the post office were as follows:

(a) collection and delivery of mail, including valued articles such as money orders and registered and insured articles;

(b) counter services, which included savings bank functions, booking of money orders, registration of letters and parcels, the sale of postage stamps, registration of broadcasting receiver licences and the selling of postal orders;

(c) receipt and despatch of telegrams, settlement of telephone bills and attending to the public call office; and

(d) control functions, including treasury and correspondence activities.

Work in the post office was typically bureaucratic, along strictly one-man, one-job lines. The control system operated at the level of customer contact, at the end of the day's work, and in preparation and submission of reports to the head office at the end of a fortnight. Each counter serving the public was designed to provide only a single service. The result was that the same customer, depending on the nature of his needs, would have to go to different counters, one after another, and, in the process, stand in line and take his turn for the particular service provided at each counter. Apart from delay, this was a cause of irritation resulting in a negative image for the postal system. The technical system of work, including work flow and social interactions, was studied jointly with the employees. The study revealed that work space was inadequate, with a high degree of congestion. For the purpose of sorting mail, for example, there was room for only six persons, although there were 14 postmen employed in the office. The congestion behind the counter was partly caused by the excessive amount of furniture, which moreover was antiquated and uncomfortable. On the other hand there was no place at the counters where members of the public could fill out forms, and no seats for elderly or infirm visitors. In addition the light sources were inadequate in themselves and improperly placed. The layout as it was in April 1975 is shown in figure 2.

It was felt that before any new form of work organisation was created, the problem of space should be resolved. Accordingly, the management decided to make available the first floor of the building to the post office by converting the residential accommodation occupied by a postal employee into office space. The space thus made available was allotted to the telegraph and public call office group, and to the entire delivery section, which consisted of three delivery clerks, one head postman and 14 postmen. Old furniture was removed and more functional pieces were brought in on both floors. The revised layouts of the two floors are shown in figures 3 and 4.

After the physical conditions of the work area had been improved, the management and the employees' representatives decided in a joint meeting that the delivery personnel would start working as a group instead of individually. They chose to have a group leader to be rotated every two weeks, so that every postman could get a chance to be group leader, mainly to provide liaison between the group and the sub-postmaster. Initially there was a leadership struggle within

Figure 2. Layout of the Chaura Maidan post office at Simla in April 1975 (Ground floor; not to scale)

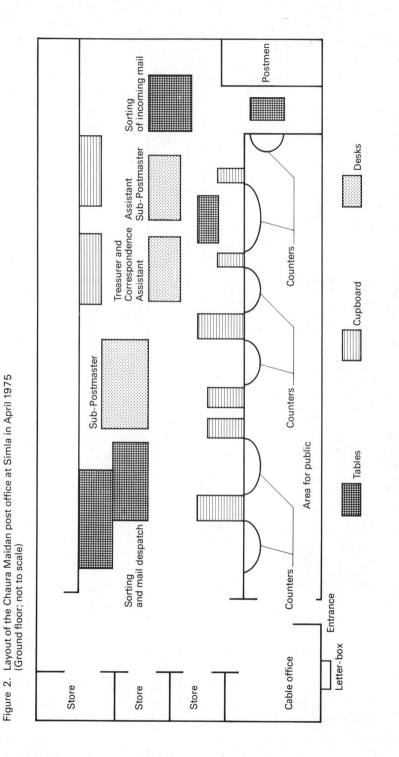

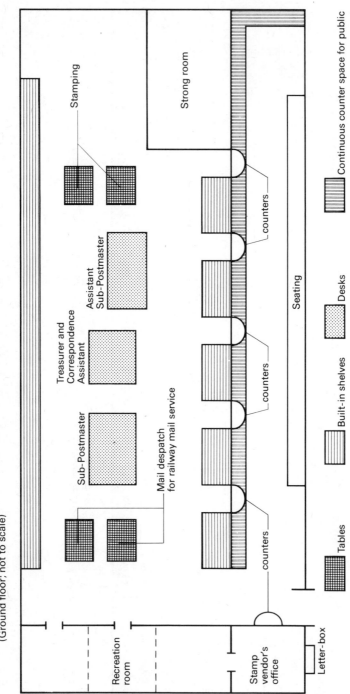

Figure 3.   Layout of the Chaura Maidan post office at Simla after work re-designing
(Ground floor; not to scale)

Figure 4. Layout of the Chaura Maidan post office at Simla after work re-designing (First floor; not to scale)

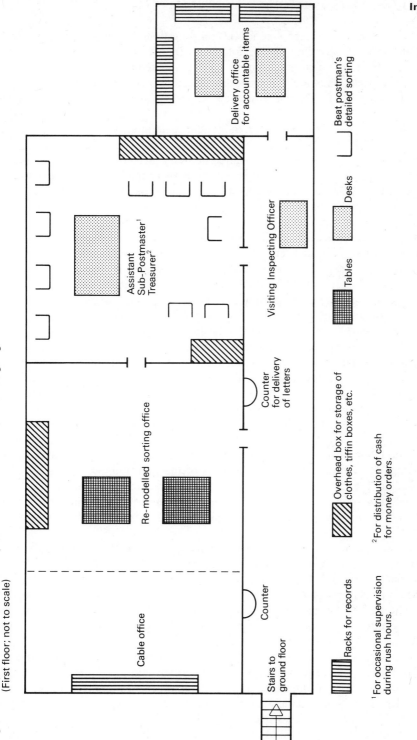

Delivery office for accountable items

Assistant Sub-Postmaster[1] Treasurer[2]

Visiting Inspecting Officer

Counter for delivery of letters

Re-modelled sorting office

Cable office

Counter

Stairs to ground floor

Beat postman's detailed sorting

Desks

Tables

Overhead box for storage of clothes, tiffin boxes, etc.

[2] For distribution of cash for money orders.

Racks for records

[1] For occasional supervision during rush hours.

the group, and there were a series of confrontations between the group and the sub-postmaster. Deciding not to intervene, the Senior Superintendent of Post Offices advised the delivery group to take up and settle all disputed issues within the group itself. Thus most of the issues affecting only the group were dealt with by the group itself, whereas any wider issue had to be taken up with the sub-postmaster.

Gradually the group learned to handle their internal conflicts and by the beginning of 1976 it began to function satisfactorily. The postmen used to bring mail from post boxes located on different beats, deface the postage stamps on letters and parcels, and close bags for the railway mail service. Under the new system both postmen and clerks started going beyond their original work assignments, with the result that if preliminary or detailed sorting work was taking too much time on a particular day, additional members would join in to expedite processing. Similarly, for accountable items such as registered letters and money orders, if the delivery clerks were unable to cope with the pressure of preparing necessary documents, the postmen themselves would volunteer their assistance. This sense of mutual help developed within the group without imposition of any directive from above. The reform of the work organisation, the creation of an integrated group for the whole task and the provision of the necessary space gave new meaning to the group's work.

Encouraged by this experience, the employees decided that the four counters meant for the public should become multiple counters, each one providing all the counter services except savings bank accounts, which was retained as a separate service provided at one counter only. There were indeed certain procedural difficulties, particularly in respect of booking of money orders, for which blank receipt forms could not be distributed among different counters. While discussing the problem with the Senior Superintendent of Post Offices, the counter group suggested that it would be possible to work out average daily money order bookings for the post office on the basis of the total number of money orders booked in the previous year. Accordingly, a predetermined number of blank receipt forms could be distributed among the four counters, and if there was a heavy rush on any particular day the sub-postmaster could take appropriate action.

It was also decided that the two telegraphers should be available to the delivery group or the counter group whenever they were free from their telegraph and related activities. The group also decided that one counter at a time should be closed on the basis of a staggered schedule in order to allow every employee to take the half-hour lunch break that was provided for in the rules but had been rarely granted in practice. Thus each employee had a legitimate lunch break while customer services were not disturbed.

Encouraged by the results of this group system of working in an otherwise highly traditional, hierarchical government organisation like this post office, the authorities decided to introduce it with the employees' support in the two other post offices in Simla, namely Chhota Simla and the Accountant-General post offices. The authorities also felt convinced that gradually the system could be introduced in other post offices in the state of Himachal Pradesh and elsewhere.

Some apprehension had been expressed earlier about the role of the three union leaders in the post office where the experiment took place. In the upshot there was leadership conflict and some confrontation between the sub-postmaster and these leaders, but gradually the group as a norm-setting and norm-enforcing agency was able to mobilise the union leaders' support in work activities. The union leaders are now perceived as helpful and constructive, a change that could not have been ensured by the traditional method.

Income-Tax Department

During a meeting of the Direct Taxes Advisory Committee early in 1975, a question was raised concerning the low work motivation of large numbers of white-collar employees, running into thousands, located in hundreds of work centres in India. It was considered desirable to alter the situation not only for the purpose of improvement in efficiency in the system of revenue assessment and collection as such but also in view of the large number of assessees involved, who often express their dissatisfaction with the delays caused by assessment formalities and consequent harassment. The meeting discussed the issue briefly and felt that a pilot project could be undertaken, preferably in the capital city of India.

Subsequently, a number of meetings took place among staff of the Directorate of Organisation and Management Services, the Income-Tax Department and the National Labour Institute. In the meantime, the Director of Management Services had attended a seminar held at the Institute on the subject of the quality of working life, and he felt that it might be a good idea to explore the possibility of a pilot project in the office of the Commissioner of Income Tax at New Delhi. Accordingly, a meeting was held at which the basic ideas of work redesign were explored with the help of illustrative examples culled from various forms of organisation of white-collar work in Europe. At that meeting it was decided to make a beginning in range II-A, where there was an assistant income-tax commissioner supervising the work of eight income-tax officers with a number of clerical employees.

The external consultants began the study in a typical room where all the records in connection with the assessees were maintained in the form of files. The layout of the room is shown in figure 5. Examination revealed that the room was congested, dingy and poorly lit (by four 100-watt bulbs). It was not regularly dusted, with the result that the files stacked almost everywhere—on shelves, on tables, on the floor—were full of dust. There was hardly space to move. The environment certainly was not conducive to work.

The work flow was also studied, jointly with the occupants, namely six record keepers and one supervisor. Each record keeper served a particular income-tax officer, for whom he maintained ledgers of various decisions, notices issued, dates fixed for meetings, etc., and saw to the normal movement of files in addition to bringing out old files whenever a dispute arose on decisions made. Besides maintaining the files, the record keepers had to attend to several registers. In addition there were two junior clerks attached to each officer, but working in separate rooms. Their work was to prepare and notify decisions on assessment

Figure 5. Layout of a record room in the Income-Tax Department

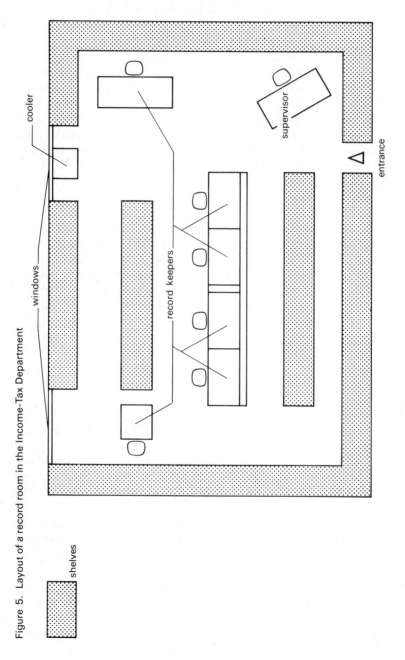

shelves

windows

cooler

record keepers

supervisor

entrance

and recovery. The supervisor had two functions: on the one hand he was expected to maintain discipline in the record room where the six record keepers had their desks, and to ensure that unauthorised persons did not enter the room and that the records were not taken out without proper authorisation; his other function was to supervise the work of four clerks attached to two officers. Because these two groups of employees worked in different rooms supervision could not be effective.

There was very little interdependence among the occupants of the room. Each record keeper was working independently, even though in close physical proximity to the others. Theoretically, if a record keeper was absent another record keeper was expected to look after his work, but this had not been happening in practice. The officers themselves took no direct interest either in the system of record maintenance itself or in the clerical personnel responsible for upkeep of the records. Some of the record keepers in fact expressed the view that since a substantial number of officers had been promoted from clerical ranks it was baffling that the officers had lost interest in the working conditions of the clerks.

In view of the sudden pressures of work in the office owing to a change of government policy it was not possible to advise the Commissioner, the Assistant Commissioner and other officers concerning the results of the study. However, a short note was prepared and sent to the Department in the hope of providing a minimum of information which could form a basis of discussion between the consultants and the Department. This note referred in particular to the following points:

(a) the possibility of integrating the job of a particular officer's record keeper with the jobs of his two junior clerks, thus forming an integrated, self-sufficient work team of the three subordinates;

(b) the possible role of the supervisor if the integrated team-work concept was accepted; and

(c) the question of layout in terms of decentralisation of records, each team of three keeping their officer's records in a self-contained room or cubicle.

In September 1976 the senior consultant from the National Labour Institute was contacted by the Commissioner. This resulted in two visits to the office—one in October and another in November 1976. The visits revealed the following changes. The original record room that had been studied and reported on had been reorganised. Changes in the physical layout had greatly improved working conditions. Some of the record keepers had been removed from the room and the congestion of records had been eliminated. The room was more airy than before. Steel racks, the desks and the chairs looked clean, tidy and more functional. Several small work centres had been formed, the record keeper and the two junior clerks being placed together wherever possible, with the records kept by their side. Each of these three-man groups had become an integrated servicing unit assisting an officer. The other record rooms had been similarly reorganised, and the congestion considerably reduced.

A review meeting was held with eight officers, the Assistant Commissioner and the Commissioner. Apart from this review, the senior consultant had informal meetings with the clerical employees. It transpired that the decentralised record-keeping and the small work teams set up had brought about a noticeably closer interdependence at work in each case between the record keeper and the clerks and between the team and the officer. This development had resulted in the more expeditious movement of files and smoother co-ordination of activities. While it was too early to judge whether the assessment cases were being disposed of quickly, the feeling of the officers was that such would be the effect in course of the coming months. The unexpected provision of minimum facilities of a functional kind, i.e. the removal of old wooden furniture and the introduction of steel racks, had constituted a distinct incentive for the clerks. The Commissioner's personal initiative along with that of the Assistant Commissioner and the income-tax officers in reorganising the system had motivated the clerical employees, whose commitment was found to be positive, in sharp contrast to what had been observed during the study conducted in 1975.

Proceeding a step further, the Department organised a series of decentralised reception centres for assessees, with comfortable furniture and reception clerks equipped with intercom telephones so that the flow of assessee traffic could be regulated in an orderly fashion. Besides earning the gratitude of the assessees, this system reduced the irritation of the junior clerks, who had in the past been unexpectedly interrupted in their work by assessees asking for information; the new system protected them against such distractions. In the past there had also been large numbers of almost totally unskilled attendants whose work had little or no meaning. Under the new system, a few attendants were posted in the reception halls, but the rest were being retrained for skilled jobs like record binding, electrical repairs and repair of furniture. This effort was also acting as an incentive for the employees in the Department.

All in all, it was found that even in a highly traditional department like the one concerned with the income tax, a redesign of the work organisation was possible and employee responsiveness could be constructively evoked so long as the responsible managers could see meaning in new forms of work and took initiative in the matter. It was proposed that the experiment from range II-A be extended to ranges II-B and II-C, two other ranges reporting to the Commissioner. It is true that no deliberate attempt had yet been made at the time of writing to foster a closer work-related team spirit through semi-autonomous group working involving job rotation. The initial steps taken, however, would tend to lead the Department step-by-step in that direction.

Hindustan Machine Tools Ltd.

Hindustan Machine Tools (HMT), a major public enterprise, has several manufacturing establishments located in different parts of the country. One of the more complex, called HMT-V, is located at Hyderabad. Among other products, it specialises in the manufacture of special-purpose machine tools.

The general manager of the plant, G. B. Appa Rao, a competent engineer known for his task orientation, had been seeking to improve its operation since he had become responsible for production activities, and had brought various innovations into being in the early 1970s. When the production target for 1974-75 was drastically raised to give over-all financial viability to the plant, and it was found necessary to optimise the utilisation of certain scarce production equipment, he introduced a novel "component centre" approach. The "component centre" concept[8] rests on the idea that components produced with a similar technology and a similar sequence of operations should be manufactured at one centre. The placing of the machines in a component centre corresponds to the sequence of operations. There is thus a simplification of the manufacturing process. In one case the advantages of the new system were—

(a) a saving in movement to the extent of 180 metres and eight occasions;

(b) inspection reduced from three times to one; and

(c) delays reduced from 16 times to zero.

After the component centre scheme had been introduced at 22 locations in the plant, a survey was undertaking in 1976[9] to determine the effectiveness of the new form of work organisation. The positive results obtained were as follows:

(1) The new approach was felt (by 62 per cent of the supervisory and managerial staff and 67 per cent of the operatives) to have simplified and improved operational layout.

(2) Machine utilisation under the new scheme reached between 75 and 80 per cent.

(3) Manufacturing cycle time showed an appreciable improvement.

(4) There was also a substantial improvement in performance. While improved performance cannot be due to a single factor, particularly when additional elements such as an incentive bonus scheme were introduced simultaneously with the component centre system, 60 per cent of supervisory and managerial personnel and 74 per cent of the operatives felt that improved performance was due to the introduction of the component centre scheme itself.

(5) It was also felt by 80 per cent of the operatives that the supervisors had become more versatile because of the varied responses their tasks entailed.

(6) Another major positive gain was found to lie in a sense of meaningfulness: the workers in a component centre could see the end product of their efforts even though an identification with the product could not be established directly.

Certain negative findings were also brought to light by the survey:

(1) The respondents felt that the pressure for target achievement was so high in each component centre that the centre put a high priority on its own task and would not respond to urgent demands from other groups. Selfishness was seen as a major factor causing delay in responding to the requirements of other component centres.

(2) Absenteeism continued to be a problem, and there was no improvement on the previous rate.

(3) Work monotony was seen as having increased: 30 per cent of the supervisory and managerial staff and 40 per cent of the operatives felt that their work was more routinised than it had been before.

(4) Records indicate that there was no appreciable quality improvement under the new system.

(5) Non-availability of tools was also regarded as a serious problem for each component centre.

The main conclusions drawn from the evaluation study in respect of the operation of the component centre system were as follows:

(1) Competitiveness among the component centres caused delays, and would have to be overcome. It would be desirable to foster co-operation.

(2) It was felt by 60 per cent of the supervisory and managerial personnel and 40 per cent of the operatives that the problem of monotony and absenteeism could be overcome by the introduction of a group system of working in the component centres instead of having each individual operating a single machine with a single specialised skill. Multi-skilling with rotational opportunities and work allocation by the group itself on internally evolved norms would make the work more attractive for operatives and supervisors.

(3) A substantial number of operatives felt that the job instructions issued tended to be excessively detailed and that they themselves could draw up operational instructions that would not lead to a reduction in product quality.

The management of the plant was seeking to take steps to rectify the negative aspects revealed in the research findings by introducing group working in the component centres.

Other cases

In India the day-to-day work experience and continuing irritation of managers have often acted as a strong spur to the development of new forms of work organisation. An example of such action is a project that was started in 1969 in the centralised cash collection centre (abbreviated as CCCC) of the *Life Insurance Corporation of India* by a young manager named R. H. Umadikar. This centre was dealing with 50,000 policies in July 1967, when computerisation was introduced and gave rise to the usual problems of resistance to change arising from the need to adapt to a new technology. Employee resistance with strong union support was a major problem that Umadikar faced as a manager.

On his own initiative, he started performing himself some of the essential tasks required by the new system, although that was not, strictly speaking, his proper function. The sincerity with which he performed the tasks brought about an initial improvement in the previously strained relations between him and his clerical employees. Gradually a group system of work evolved as the employees became interested and then involved in studying the new technological demands calling for creation of an appropriate work organisation. Umadikar and his clerical employees working together ultimately designed and successfully applied a new system. A report[10] was prepared in 1969 which received commendation from the then chairman of the company. The report gives the impression that Umadikar's activities took the form of action-research, i.e. the use of techniques of social and psychological research to identify social problems in a group or community, coupled with active participation of the investigator in group efforts to solve those problems. The resulting new form of work organisation could simultaneously provide for technological demands and constructive employee responses.

A similar effort is reported from the *Neyveli Lignite Corporation,* a public-sector undertaking near Madras with 17,500 employees. The corporation is concerned with mining lignite, operation of a large thermal power-generating station, the manufacture of fertiliser and briquettes and carbonisation. It has had a long history of disturbed operations and a chequered industrial relations background: at one stage its personnel included members of more than two dozen registered trade unions, of which six were still active in 1976.

Under the late S. M. Kumaramangalam, a dynamic minister of the Government of India, there was a leadership change in this undertaking in 1971, with infusion of new blood at the top. While the situation was gradually improving, in late 1974, a young administrator was appointed director of personnel. In early 1975 the Corporation decided, on the basis of his diagnosis of the problems of productivity as well as worker motivation, to break away from the work system based on compartmentalisation. Since then it has been possible to introduce in the central workshop, the foundry, the thermal power station and at the open-cast mining site a multi-skilled system with a view to giving a greater sense of responsibility and satisfaction to each worker on the job. In the machine shop, for example, almost every worker is skilled in two trades if not in three; in the foundry shop a core-maker also does the work of a moulder; similarly, fitters, welders, riggers, blacksmiths, turners and machine operators in various shops have become multi-skilled. This effort at job enrichment carried out over a period of 18 months was matched by an appropriate group production incentive scheme. The result was some semblance of group functioning, though at a more rudimentary level than in either the Tiruchirapalli or the Hardwar unit of Bharat Heavy Electricals. None the less, employees' involvement in the new work system was visibly greater than it had been before. An evaluation in October 1976 revealed that workers were more satisfied because they felt that they had acquired some control over the work process.

Other similar cases can be cited. The essential cause of such spontaneous efforts is usually the sensivity of some perceptive managers, who realise that often the traditional form of work organisation is not congruent with the informal social system of work. On the basis of their practical experience, they therefore try to bring new forms of work organisation into being in their own way. External consultants have not played any role in these kinds of projects.

Seminars organised by the National Labour Institute since 1974 on the re-design of work and the quality of working life have also prompted a number of projects. Some of the managerial personnel attending these seminars (or "workshops") have taken the initiative in examining their own work systems with a view to reorganising them by a participative design method. One such case already reported is that of the Tiruchirapalli unit of Bharat Heavy Electricals. A second case is that of the *Pinjore factory of Hindustan Machine Tools.* This machine tool factory sent its production manager, D. K. Chakravorty, to one of the Institute's workshops. When he returned he studied the work system of the accessories shop where some key parts are manufactured for the main machine tool unit. There are two major operations involved, buffing and assembling. At the time of his investigation these two operations were being done by two different sets of workers. The usual Taylorian rationale assumed that this kind of division of labour would bring about efficiency in operation. In his experience, however, persistent absenteeism was causing problems of redeployment of the workforce, and in the case of the younger workers the monotony of the tasks was reducing efficiency. So he arranged a series of problem-solving discussions with 21 workers, and gradually the idea emerged that the same worker, with some training, would be able to deal with both buffing and assembling operations. The group also felt that since the accessories were of different types they could be classified accordingly and small groups of workers could handle different types on a planned rotational basis. When the system was introduced productivity gradually improved in terms both of quantity and of quality, and after 18 months it was found possible to deploy seven workers elsewhere in the factory since 14 were found to be enough for the job. The only help that Chakravorty sought from the National Labour Institute was documentary information on cases of redesign of work systems.

The more obvious way of initiating a project is for external consultants to be involved in it from the beginning, co-operating with the managers, trade union leaders and workers concerned, and helping them gradually to evolve a participative system in laying the foundation for new forms of work organisation. This is how the Hardwar project started. In monitoring the progress of a demonstration project, however, different systems have been followed at different sites. At one location, for example, the progress was being continuously monitored by an internal change agent, an engineer and behavioural scientist engaged in social science research; only for external advice was a research worker from the National Labour Institute called in. Encouraged by the experience, the organisation is proposing to initiate the process at three other sites, this time relying entirely on the internal change agent.

In another organisation the external consultants are involved at each stage of the demonstration project. There are monthly review meetings with the task force to review progress as well as to examine the further steps that are being planned. In the case of the Hardwar unit the external consultants are also involved, on a month-to-month basis, not so much in review of what a group is doing but in diffusing the experience acquired to other shops. However, there are definite signs that internal change agents are gradually taking over this role.

Another relevant case is that of *Engineers, India,* a well known consulting firm specialising in oil refining and the manufacture of chemical fertilisers. Under the leadership of its first chairman this public enterprise rapidly developed its activities and strengthened its workforce, mostly consisting of young engineers and technicians. As is often the case when a strong personality is at the helm, the work system was a dual one, personal relations with scientists and technologists contrasting with a bureaucratic work structure for the lower grades of employees.

Certain disconcerting developments towards the end of the chairman's tenure were greeted first with disbelief and then with shock on his part since he had always thought of himself as a benevolent taskmaster and had expected appreciation for all he had done for the growth of business and the benefit of the employees. However, he did realise that with the lower levels of employees groaning under a tight procedural system, certain elements of freedom had to be provided. Several departmental committees were set up but, as is usual in an atmosphere of mistrust and unwillingness to share information, the workings of this consultative machinery became another frustrating experience.

In the meantime, the personnel manager had tried to restructure the work system in the organisation. Several seminars had been held with the scientists and technologists, without much success. When the founding chairman left, a new chairman was appointed who did not have adequate time for the company because he had another major assignment. A high degree of anxiety prevailed, particularly among young engineers. There was also a considerable degree of frustration at the senior level where people were working more on their own rather than as members of a team.

The personnel manager decided to start action within his own staff of 13 members. In October 1976 all of them, from the manager down to the typists, held a full-day discussion meeting. The day's exploration identified three task-related subgroups within the personnel staff, dealing respectively with training and development, industrial relations, and communication systems. Certain preliminary redesigning of the three task structures was carried out. Thereafter, the personnel staff held four exploratory meetings until the first week of December 1976. It was found that certain work readjustments were taking place on other bases, and the original concept of three task-related subgroups was discarded.

On the whole, the impression of the external consultant concerned with this case was that the personnel staff wanted to maintain its identity as a close-knit unit in relation to the prestigious groups of technological staff. It would not have liked to run the risk of creating task-related subgroups, the apprehension being that such action might further erode whatever collective identity the personnel staff had. This is an interesting example of the initiation process. The conclusion to be drawn from it is that while the application of advanced knowledge, as in this engineering consulting firm, demands a flexible work system, the spirit of Taylorism was so fixed in the minds of its top managers that they were unable to trace the symptoms of employee discontent to the root cause, namely the bureaucratic organisation of work. The personnel manager started with this own staff because there he had enough elbow room.

GENERAL CONCLUSIONS

A number of preliminary comments need to be made before embarking on even a tentative evaluation of Indian experience of new forms of work organisation. In the first place, it is of interest to note that all available information on Indian experiments, barring the very first one in Ahmedabad, comes from public undertakings and government systems. There is no ongoing project in the private sector. Secondly, it may be noted that some of the transnational corporations like Imperial Chemical Industries and Shell, which have experimented with new forms of work organisation at their home bases,[11] have not taken any meaningful steps in that direction in India. It is a matter for speculation whether in the developing countries transnational corporations have taken any initiative towards research into new forms of (local) work organisation. Indian experience suggests that the transnationals are glued to Weber-Taylor traditions in their work organisation, regarding the values of an "economic man" as the primary force in work motivation, the appropriate instrumentality thus being union-management bargaining.

Pattern of development of individual projects

The Indian cases were discussed in detail with some of the internal consultants in early December 1976. From the discussion one can trace certain elements that are common to many of the cases reported. The general development pattern found in the Indian cases is as follows.

(1) At the initial stage, when the experiment begins, there is a feeling among employees, irrespective of their positions and roles and despite preliminary explorations, discussions and clarifications sought and offered, that the experiment is motivated by the management's desire to gain or by the research worker's desire to conduct research in order to publish the results. Internal consultants are seen as motivated by career considerations. There is a high degree of selective perception of cases of failure not necessarily related to experiments with new forms of work organisation but to other past efforts to bring about any change—technological or other—in the system. Cases of success are not remembered or mentioned. In most Indian cases this hostility has not been openly manifested, but overt expression of hostility has often come from isolated individuals. At this stage there is hardly any sign of a desire to know more about the experiments with a view to democratising the workplace.

(2) At the next stage some degree of curiosity develops but there is no sign of commitment, although a few persons involved in the experiment apparently feel that some changes for the better can be made. Positive leaders among the experimental groups do play an important role in this phase as well as in the earlier phase.

(3) At the third stage a substantial number of people show interest in what is happening, seeking information, taking the initiative in group discussion and offering suggestions, while the majority are ambivalent, not being sure whether the work situation is improving or not.

(4) At a fourth stage the attention received makes the participants in the experiment feel privileged, while other members of the workforce harbour a feeling of jealousy and some hostility, often expressed by way of jokes and caustic comments.

(5) At the next stage group consciousness brings some degree of stability to the experimental group; on the other hand there is an internal power struggle, at times aggravated by caste and regional considerations, between subgroups

with negative, positive and intermediate attitudes towards the experiment. The positive subgroups now take a more active interest and gradually assume control functions in the autonomous groups.

(6) At the next stage the majority of the participants, having experienced some positive gains, at least in some key respects such as variety of job, meaningfulness, social support, challenge, autonomy, and evolving norms for the group, are already committed to the experiment. The negative elements are isolated, and depending on how the majority treats them, they indicate either withdrawal of a passive kind or personal hostility. By and large, however, the group settles down to work out the operational details of the scheme at this stage.

(7) At a subsequent stage an experimental group takes the initiative of looking outwards, seeking to compare notes and experience with other similar groups, and there is thus a potential for diffusion.

While the phases outlined above could overlap and the sequence was by no means strictly followed in all the cases reported, the phases do appear to highlight the dynamics of change as perceived by the internal consultants, although at times not apparent to the external consultants. A relevant factor is the size of the group; depending on the task system, optimum size could be important.

Patterns of diffusion

The diffusion process has two related aspects. First, knowledge of new forms of work organisation has to be spread among an increasing number of persons—managers and administrators, trade union leaders and researchers. Secondly, demonstration projects should spread from one site to another within an existing organisation, and from one such organisation to another, until whole sectors of organised activity are covered. The clear visibility of sequential stages of success is an important factor in enabling an experiment to gather momentum. The Hardwar case, the Chaura Maidan post office case and the Tiruchirapalli case indicate that the regular publication of some key results has been of considerable help in putting projects on a firm basis. The example of the demonstration projects in Blocks V and II at Hardwar has been followed at other work sites (including in that case the personnel department). At Tiruchirapalli the successful demonstration projects in two production shops were duplicated in the production planning and materials management departments. At the central foundry forge plant, because the plant itself is entirely new, new forms of work organisation appear to have the potential of enterprise-wise diffusion, even though one cannot be sure of the outcome at this early stage. The postal case, unlike the income-tax case, is already leading to planned demonstrations at other post offices located in the same region, with the possibility that in coming years the changes may spread to many more post offices in various parts of the country.

It is also worth while to look at the diffusion process in terms of the experts who take part in it. The initial projects in the early 1950s at Ahmedabad started with A. K. Rice. Some of his colleagues from the Tavistock Institute of Human Relations were involved in the project along with him, and no doubt there were some Indian social scientists as well. There was no purposeful plan, however, for systematically diffusing the results of the project. Accordingly, when Rice left, there was nobody to assume the responsibility of carrying the lessons of the Ahmedabad experiment to other areas. Another lesson, from the evaluation study of Miller referred to earlier,[2] is that the internal management response did not develop sufficiently, with the consequence that the demonstration project could continue until the time of writing at only one of the four project sites.

These lessons have been taken into account by the staff of the National Labour Institute. From the beginning, one of their objectives was that among the leaders involved in each demonstration project, individuals belonging to trade unions and management should be singled out to pursue the effort within their own organisation and to be available also to other organisations if the opportunity arose. The Hardwar unit has, for example, a dozen employees, including some trade union leaders, who have acquired substantial knowledge and skill with regard to diffusion. In the post office department there are three such persons. At the Tiruchirapalli unit there are half a dozen and a continuous effort is being made to increase the number. On the other hand the response among social scientists with a bent for research continues to be poor. Perhaps the reason is that academics are apt to prefer lecturing, discussion with colleagues and students and documentary research to the frequent rough give-and-take of action-research.

Consultants' role

Practically all the external consultants and most of the internal consultants involved in the Indian cases had previous experience of organisation development work. However, they tended to find that such work, dealing with people in abstraction from their tasks, did not provide adequate satisfaction, and they were being steadily drawn to the socio-technical systems approach. The consultant's role in promoting participation should be obvious, namely to facilitate the democratic development of new work forms, from diagnosis to planning, implementation, stabilisation and diffusion. There are a number of variations in this basic role. In the first place, a broad distinction can be drawn between the roles of the external and the internal consultant. An internal consultant is very often assisted by external consultants to acquire the skills and confidence that are required in initiating work redesign projects. The relationship, therefore, is often a complementary one of mutual esteem and trust. This was the case in respect of the Hardwar unit and the Chaura Maidan post office. In some other cases the internal consultants have managerial responsibilities and consequently cannot find adequate time for the project, which also lacks the autonomy that is essential at the initial stage.

Yet another case is provided by the HMT component centre experiment. M. S. S. Varadan and his group were allowed to carry out an evaluation study as internal consultants, but the enterprise was somewhat hesitant to allow him and his colleagues to become involved in a work redesign demonstration project. It is still not very clear whether the data derived from their research will now permit them to be more actively involved in an action-research role that has so far been denied to them.

The Indian cases show that although external consultants gradually become redundant once a project is under way they can still have a role to play in the diffusion process. Two of the more successful cases—the Hardwar unit of Bharat Heavy Electricals and the post office—provide examples of this dependence. On the other hand for the diffusion of new forms of work organisation the Scandinavian countries and Australia have in recent years adopted a network strategy, under which there is less dependence on external consultants or researchers and more interaction among the experimental units, each learning from the others. This participative design process will not necessarily make external consultants completely redundant, but will certainly change their role drastically. In Indian conditions this option seems to have some hope of success. The external consultants who have been active since 1973 are steadily re-examining and evaluating their role in relation to the internal consultants, and are gradually making it possible for the latter to take charge of the diagnosis, design, implementation, evaluation and diffusion of projects.

Role of the supervisor

The role of supervisory personnel in any organisational innovation including training and development has been discussed at length in writings on this subject. The roles that are emerging for the middle managers at the Indian experimental sites have a number of common features.

(1) The intensity and quality of interaction between the supervisory personnel of the experimental groups and their counterparts in other departments have invariably increased. In practically all the cases the interaction has been positive, except perhaps in the case of the HMT component centres, which are plagued by competitive relationships.

(2) The supervisory personnel have been involved in somewhat longer-term planning, which has given a stamp of distinction to their position. In units like the Tiruchirapalli and Hardwar plants of Bharat Heavy Electricals supervisory personnel have found themselves more and more involved in production planning and in scheduling programmes for a period of two to four weeks.

(3) The control function of the supervisors had undergone a change, although not in equal measure in all cases. The extent of the change is conditioned partly by the supervisor's leadership qualities and partly by the ability of the experimental group to develop internal norms of work, including handling of the problem of discipline. At the Tiruchirapalli plant the supervisory role in control is perceptibly diminished, whereas this is not so in the case of the HMT component centre; at the Hardwar plant and the Chaura Maidan post office an intermediate stage had been reached.

(4) The supervisors' interest in their own development had increased perceptibly in most of the cases. They now saw their own training and developmental needs in a better perspective than they had been able to see them before. At the Hardwar unit of Bharat Heavy Electricals, for example, there had been specific requests from the supervisory personnel from all experimental sites

indicating that they would like to undergo training in planning and co-ordination functions as well as to acquire the ability to undertake technical and social analysis of work systems.

It is pertinent to mention here that there are cases of individual supervisors who have not been able to adjust to an experiment. One representative case is provided by an old supervisor in one of the production centres of the Hardwar unit. With his long experience of a tight-fisted supervisory style, he simply could not adjust even though the management was aware of his difficulties and tried to help him during the painful process of readjustment to the new role. The efforts did not succeed, and ultimately it was necessary to transfer the supervisor to a job where he would not have to face such difficulties.

Role of the existing top leadership

The character of the existing organisation, as reflected in the over-all leadership of management and labour on the one hand, and their inter-relationships on the other, is an important factor in generating interest in work redesign. It is also relevant to the diffusion process. In the income-tax case, for example, a note prepared by the external consultant appealed to the Commissioner of Income Tax, and repeated action on his part and that of his colleagues resulted in the introduction of a modular system of work organisation as described earlier. In a traditional hierarchical organisation, this kind of approach can be effective, particularly where there is no strong trade union movement. In the Hardwar factory, on the other hand, the leaders of the unit were playing a supportive role without direct involvement. The General Manager (Production) and his counterpart in the administration, two key men next to the Executive Director, were also involved in an indirect way, through contact with the external consultants rather than in the day-to-day working out of the project. The shop managers and supervisors were thus given an opportunity to operate autonomously on the demonstration sites as members of the task forces. This type of approach was conceivable at the Hardwar unit, with a more open and comparatively more democratic functioning of the managerial system, but not at the income-tax office. Yet it would be rather premature to conclude that one approach will work for government and another approach for industry. For example, unlike the Commissioner of Income Tax, the Senior Superintendent of Post Offices and the Director of Postal Training, who are in much higher positions than the sub-postmaster and his subordinates in the Chaura Maidan post office, played an indirect supportive role, eschewing a direct involvement in the change process.

On the whole, therefore, it is difficult to identify any aspect of organisation influence in India as being of critical importance for the success of a project. In negative terms, opposition or total apathy at the top level will harm any effort to change. In positive terms, management at one or two levels above the committed parties, if definitely supportive, can be a substantial help.

Role of trade unions

In respect of the trade unions the Indian cases reported fall roughly into two categories, according to whether the unions are strong or weak. At the Hardwar and Tiruchirapalli units of Bharat Heavy Electricals, for example, the trade union movement was quite strong, although both the units had multiple unions organised along political lines. Here again, there is a difference. At the Tiruchirapalli unit, there was a tradition of harmonious union-management relations and the union was not opposed to work redesign schemes as such in the drum shop and the header shop, although the recognised trade union had not been actively involved in the project. At the Hardwar unit, on the other hand, relations in the past had been strained, and inter-union rivalry persisted. For this reason the external consultants had been obliged to spend, in the initial period, a considerable amount of time with the leaders of rival trade unions explaining the objectives of the experiment in terms of the workers' new role and the new opportunities for them. Occasionally, joint meetings with the unions and management were also necessary.

In other cases the trade unions are either weak or uninterested in the demonstration projects, partly because of the low-key beginning of the project and partly because of the lack of interest of the union leaders in work-related issues and apathy towards work and work life. At the Chaura Maidan post office three union leaders had initial difficulties in adjusting to the group-based working system but were gradually persuaded to appreciate the advantages of increased elbow-room for the performance of otherwise unchallenging jobs, and became committed to the project.

On the whole, the Indian data so far indicate that grass-roots trade union leaders who have been involved in demonstration projects have not only responded positively, but are also playing a role in diffusion efforts, as at the Hardwar unit. At the national level, however, the trade union leadership is still not involved in the process of overcoming work alienation, and continues to be chiefly concerned with bargainable issues.

Reward structure

In India it is definitely more complicated to create new forms of work organisation if the existing organisation is plagued by a high degree of frustration among employees and if they have a strong negative image of the organisation. The immediate establishment of better reward structures would be an important requirement in such cases. However, the designing of appropriate reward structures continues to be an unresolved problem in India. It remains unresolved because there are too many variables that make the picture overly complex. For example, if the existing organisation provides openings for corruption, the resistance to developing new forms of work organisation is stronger than it would be otherwise. This fact is often not perceived by external or internal consultants because corruption is not a subject for open exploration.

Another example of the difficulties involved in changing reward structures is provided by the Hardwar unit. It has a group reward scheme, which, by itself, would have been satisfactory to the groups working on work redesign demonstration sites. Unfortunately, however, in the other shops the continuing practice of overtime payments for extra work done is obviously so advantageous for the workers concerned that at times the workers who have volunteered for the participative system are puzzled about the inequities of the reward structure. Production shortfalls, partly if not mainly caused by the traditional work system, encourage overtime working, and a vicious circle is established. There is no such problem at the Tiruchirapalli unit of Bharat Heavy Electricals, where various forms of tangible and intangible rewards directly related to efforts and performance were introduced: from the very beginning due acknowledgement was made for all the elements contributing to team work in the plant, with the result that the whole reward structure was seen to be fair and equitable.

For the government service, as in the post office and the income-tax office, there is little, if any, scope for financial rewards for being multi-skilled or for accepting the socio-technical system of work organisation. There are some reward schemes in the Income-Tax Department but hardly any in the postal service. In the Income-Tax Department the employees' team spirit was strengthened by the change of physical layout and by forming work-related groups around each income-tax officer. Similarly, a drastic change in the physical layout at Chaura Maidan post office, with sufficient interest taken in the project by the senior officers, were felt by the postmen and the counter clerks as a significant expression of the care and concern of the authorities. These factors contributed, in no mean measure, to developing group consciousness among the postmen and, later on, among the counter clerks.

A bigger issue in respect of designing an appropriate compensation system is that even where the management and the workers concerned are committed to developing a reward system for the employees involved on experimental sites they are often hesitant to take any action because the non-experimental shops might react adversely to such steps. If a project could quickly be extended throughout an enterprise, there might be no difficulty in developing appropriate reward structures. Yet another issue that was being debated at the Hardwar plant is whether workers should be rewarded for acquiring additional skills or whether a reward should be conditional on the utilisation of the skills in question. If the utilisation of skills becomes the objective, an enterprise is confronted with a new challenge, namely to achieve a higher level of sophistication in the redesign of the work system. In such a case the redesign affects the higher supervisory and managerial functions, and the human potential activated under the new scheme of things can be utilised in ordinary work situations devoid of the novelty of experimental projects.

Practical scope for real innovation

A noteworthy aspect of the Indian cases seems to be an inability to utilise to the best advantage the full range of possibilities within an enterprise. The experiments that have been carried out in the offices or in production shops are still somewhat restricted by structural limitations of the organisations themselves. The particular approach adopted at the Hardwar unit seems to have spread to several other experimental sites, but this spread may be simply due to reluctance to look into other possibilities. There are cases reported in which more emphasis has been placed on individual job enrichment than on autonomous group functioning. However, while it may be unreasonable to expect Volvo-type innovation in work organisation to emerge in India, the spirit of innovation shown in designing a work system in a children's school, Shishu Vihar,[12] could be more productively explored in different situations. There is a danger that as the quality of working life movement becomes a new fashion, almost like organisation development in the 1960s, the scope for innovation may be reduced.

Evaluation criteria

The efficacy of new forms of work organisation cannot be clearly assessed except in relation to specific criteria. In all countries there is a conflict, explicit or implicit, between productivity and human criteria. Productivity criteria still dominate the world at work, crushingly so in the developing countries. The concept of surplus has a magic halo around it. The goal orientation of an enterprise is perhaps the most important factor leading to a decision to undertake experiments with new forms of work organisation. By and large, however, the workers also seek to assess experiments with new forms of work organisation in productivity terms because it is thus easier to deal with the question of financial rewards. Even social scientists are essentially concerned with measuring productivity before and after an experiment. But what of the well-being of the worker and his family? The concept of well-being remains elusive, difficult to define. More importantly, organisational experiments in India have so far not succeeded in establishing a meaningful connection between productivity and human well-being. Only in the Hardwar case did the management definitely seek information about the state of the total system by measuring the quality of working life, the quality of family life, the quality of community life and the dynamics of their interaction.

The cases presented indicate that the experiments with new forms of work organisation have proved their worth in terms of traditional productivity criteria. In this connection it should be pointed out that participative design will take due account of certain factors that tend to be neglected under a traditional industrial engineering approach. In the case of the post office, for example, when the working of the system was being diagnosed, it became obvious that precious space was being occupied by old records which, under the regulations, could have been discarded long ago. It is interesting to note that whereas the organisation and method study group, which operates on the premise of Tayloristic principles, suggested a complement of 45 employees for the Chaura Maidan post office, once the work system had been redesigned on a participative basis the number needed was reduced to 39.

Another weakness of traditional concepts of productivity measurement emerged at the Hardwar plant, where it became evident that the traditional concept of the primacy of direct labour on the work piece was questionable because in a fabrication shop where the movement of heavy materials was essentially regulated by overhead electrical cranes the crane operator and his colleagues, the slingers, made as significant a contribution to productivity as workers directly engaged in fabrication. Thus, an integrated concept of measurement developed under which equal importance was attached to what had traditionally been distinguished as direct or indirect labour.

Quality of life and work

However, it would be a mistake to rely exclusively on productivity criteria to evaluate the quality of working life. As already mentioned, the redesign of the work system in the Income-Tax Department involved the creation of decentralised work centres around income-tax officers. That resulted in productivity increases in terms of a quicker rate of assessment and disposal of files, and this is certainly an impressive indicator. Should the senior officers concerned view these achievements as fulfilment of their objectives, however, then the demonstration project would to some extent have failed in its purpose: it is important to look also at other aspects, especially the team work criteria. One significant effect emerging from the Indian cases is an awareness that new forms of work organisation are not inspired by Taylorism. Steadily gaining acceptance as the rationale for new forms of work organisation is an awareness that there can be no meaningful improvement in the quality of working life unless management of the exclusively authoritarian type is superseded by a genuine participation of the parties concerned, that the tyranny of technology should be tamed by flexibility in work forms, that hierarchical control should give way to appropriate forms of self-regulation and control through autonomous or semi-autonomous group working and that, in the end, working men and women should be measured as creators of meaningful work rather than as instruments of production.

The question of quality of life is as ancient as recorded history. In the Greek city-states, for example, the concept of quality of life was discussed by philosophers, but it was based on the institution of slavery. Today slavery is perhaps rare, and is indeed an object of universal condemnation. In any event, however, the quality of life in general is still based on the quality of working life, which is a major derivative of the form of work organisation. In the early 1930s Antonio Gramsci, while deliberating on the consequences of Taylorism, observed that "quality should be attributed to men, not to things; and human quality is raised and refined to the extent that man can satisfy a greater number of needs and thus make himself independent of them".[13] The concern for the "human content" of work led him to the far-sighted vision of the "collective worker" and the factory council. In a similar vein, after almost half a century, Herbst declared that "the product of work is people".[14] His further observation that "the learning system should be work-oriented and the work system should be learning-oriented" provides a dramatic summing up of the ongoing quest for new systems of work design that can motivate men and women to strive for higher ideals, without which human beings will remain mere instruments of production.

Notes

[1] A. K. Rice: *Productivity and social organization: The Ahmedabad Experiment: Technical innovation, work organization and management* (London, Tavistock Publications, 1958).

[2] Eric J. Miller: "Socio-technical systems in weaving, 1953-1970: A follow-up study", in *Human Relations*, May 1975, pp. 349-386.

[3] Raised, for example, in relation to Sweden, the United Kingdom and the United States, in Nancy Foy and Herman Gadon: "Worker participation: Contrasts in three countries", in *Harvard Business Review,* May-June 1976, pp. 71-83.

[4] W. W. van Groenou: "Sociology of work in India", in G. R. Gupta (ed.): *Main currents in Indian sociology,* Vol. I (Delhi, Vikas Publishing House, 1976).

[5] See Mason Haire et al.: *Managerial thinking* (New York, McGraw-Hill, 1966), and Bernard Smith et al.: "Cross-cultural attitudes among managers: A case study", in *Sloan Management Review,* Spring 1972.

[6] Vijay Rukmini Rao: *Identification of training needs for supervisory personnel at Hardwar Unit* (New Delhi, National Labour Institute, 1976; mimeographed).

[7] idem: "Quality of life in an industrial township: An initial survey", in *National Labour Institute Bulletin* (New Delhi), Oct. 1975, pp. 8-12.

[8] G. B. Appa Rao: *Component centre concept in HMT-V* (Bangalore, Hindustan Machine Tools Limited, 1975; mimeographed).

[9] M. S. S. Varadan et al.: *An opinion study of the component centre system at HMT* (Bangalore, HMT Centre for Manpower Development and Research, 1976; mimeographed).

[10] R. H. Umadikar: *The CCCC story* (Bombay, Life Insurance Corporation of India, 1969; mimeographed).

[11] On Imperial Chemical Industries, see Vol. 1 of the present work, pp. 121-128.

[12] Vijay Rukmini Rao: "Shishu Vihar: An evolving learning system", in *National Labour Institute Bulletin,* Aug. 1976, pp. 288-294.

[13] Antonio Gramsci: *Selections from the prison notebooks* (New York, International Publishers, 1973).

[14] Title of a paper contributed to a conference on the quality of working life held at Harriman, New York, in 1972. The author's proposition is explained in the following passages, in particular:

"The significance of what we do is not always evident while we are doing it. As children, most of us were absorbed in various games either by ourselves or with others. At the time we were intensely involved in what we were doing, which we took to be an aim in itself. It is only in retrospect that we are able to recognize that we were then developing qualities that were needed to help us to make the passage into adulthood.

"The same can be said of the tasks we engage in during the adult phase of our life. . . .

". . . As we begin to enter the post-adult period . . . , that which appeared to be the product begins to be seen almost as a by-product. . . . That which we have achieved is always in the past, and as soon as it is achieved it is no longer truly related to us. However, that which we have become—our qualities as human beings and our potential for future development—is always in the here and now. After everything else is gone, that which we have become remains, whether we recognize this or not, as the product.

"The products of our adult life are rather like a shell that protects the growth of the fruit that is inside. As soon as one realizes that the shell that one has produced is not that which is of essential value, one may discover and make use of what one finds in oneself. . . .

"If we speak today of the developed part of the world, what we find in the Western world is a high level of development in terms of what provides satisfaction but not in terms of understanding how to overcome distress. Satisfaction derives from whatever can be obtained from the environment, and our society is geared to achieve this. However, contentment, peace of mind, happiness, and wisdom—these are not obtainable from the environment in the same way, but are found in oneself, and to achieve them involves a different form of work. . . ." (Reproduced in P. G. Herbst: *Socio-technical design: Strategies in multidisciplinary research* (London, Tavistock Publications, 1974), pp. 212-213 and 216.)

ITALY

ITALY
Alessandro Fantoli*

NATIONAL CONDITIONS

Peculiarities of the Italian situation

In Italy new forms of work organisation became a major issue as a result of the industrial strife which started in 1968 and built up to a peak in the autumn of 1969. These origins have had marked practical and ideological consequences, in the sense that because the issue sprang from the grass roots of mass action the connection between labour and the organisation of work was rightly seen from the first as being a question of structure and not merely as a matter for psychological and sociological inquiry. Moreover, this background, which is peculiar to the Italian scene, has given rise to original research on the part of management and labour with a view to the elaboration of hypotheses, principles and approaches that will correspond to the facts of the matter. In this connection special mention should be made of the research carried out by INTERSIND (the employers' association of the IRI group of undertakings in which there is an element of state ownership), the Olivetti Company and the trade unions.[1]

In view of the circumstances described above, it seems useful to outline the concepts which appear to govern the Italian approach to the organisation of work.[2] These concepts are as follows. First of all, the production process can be represented as a combination of the main elements that enter into it, viz. technology, labour and organisation, and its efficiency can be measured by input-output analysis. However different they may have appeared to be on the surface, recent developments in all industrialised countries (e.g. the events of May 1968 in France, the above-mentioned industrial strife in Italy in 1968-69, absenteeism and labour turnover in Scandinavia) have been similar in many ways. In particular they have demonstrated that the fundamental factors in production are technology and labour, while organisation can be regarded as the factor ensuring optimisation of the above-mentioned two major factors in different social and economic contexts.

In more concrete terms this demonstration rests on the following historical development. For successive decades during the spread of industrialisation, there was an abundance of manual workers who could easily be harnessed to the

---

* Member of the Board of ARPES (Analisi ricerche piani economici e sociali), Rome.

changing needs of technological and organisational systems. This abundant supply ensured that labour had very little bargaining power, and could therefore be treated as a dependent variable. Conversely, the characteristics of the labour supply (in terms of education, skill, differentiation in rates of pay, unionisation) have now changed so that the bargaining power of labour has grown and labour has become an independent variable. This change has brought about changes in investment (location, scale, layout, environmental conditions, mechanisation) and in the organisation of work (horizontal and vertical division of labour, work pace, control).

It has thus become apparent that there are no "objective" factors governing work performance (price, duration, work pace, job content, etc.): it depends on the labour market (that is, on the demographic, economic and educational factors that produce variations in the quantity and quality of labour) and on the relative strength of employers and workers. In other words, there is no predetermined relationship between technology and the organisation of work: particular kinds of technology do not, necessarily or even with a high degree of probability, correspond to specified models of work organisation. No initial choice in respect of work organisation is ever dictated by the choice of technology.

The fact is that the development of productive forces modifies their relationship. For example recent changes in work organisation tend essentially towards a better utilisation of the increased potential of the workforce, but that same increase in potential explains the drive for a change in the social division of labour, a reduction of inequalities connected with individual tasks, and changes in the distribution of control over the production process. Thus an egalitarian movement accentuates the incongruity of the division of authority and functions inherent in scientific management.

Economic and social trends

In the 1950s the Italian economy was still predominantly agricultural, and agriculture accounted for about 40 per cent of the gainfully employed population. At the end of that decade, however (from 1959 to 1969), the north of Italy witnessed a spurt of industrialisation, particularly in the manufacture of mechanical products (motor cars, household appliances, etc.) and textiles (both fabrics and clothing). This development was based on the employment of workers from the agricultural sector: millions of workers left the land (particularly in the south of the country, where there was much poverty) and moved to the areas where industrialisation was highly concentrated. This was the time of the Italian "economic miracle" based on a labour-intensive work structure, low wages and low productivity.

Industrialisation and regional concentration went so fast as to cause a bottleneck in the labour market and a rise in wages which threatened to make production uneconomic. To survive the crisis that occurred in 1964, industry endeavoured to achieve higher productivity not by investing in new technology but through scientific management to increase the output of the individual worker. Management was thus led to restrict its choice of labour to men, preferably married and relatively educated, between 25 and 40 years of age. The urban and industrial labour market was thus closed to women, young people, older people and the relatively uneducated. This choice reduced the potential supply of labour, so that supply also became somewhat inelastic. The increased rigidity of the labour market can be attributed to two factors. First, a growing number of young people stayed on longer at school, so that there were fewer young manual workers and an abundance of young non-manuals. Secondly, industrial plants are concentrated in the big towns of northern Italy, where housing, transport and social services have turned out to be inadequate for the number of incoming migrants; the lack of child welfare services, in particular, prevents women from entering the labour market (the labour force participation rate is the lowest in Europe) while the shortage of housing and of transport facilities makes life difficult for workers' families, particularly where, as in the majority of cases, only the head of the family has a steady job. The Italian labour market is thus divided into three segments: urban industrial employment, casual manual employment and non-manual employment.[3] The second of these is independent and self-perpetuating, and does not provide a pool of reserve labour for the first, largely because the supply in the second is essentially one of part-time, seasonal or home workers only.[4]

Thus in spite of widespread underemployment throughout the country, when business improved in 1968-69 the labour supply remained very inelastic in the urban industrial sector of employment, and the workers and trade unions found themselves in an extraordinarily strong position. To overcome its labour shortage, industry began to decentralise by entrusting part of the production process to formally independent units (even having recourse to home work), and this strengthened the casual labour market, in which a combination of part-time agricultural work, industrial home work and seasonal migration for employment in construction and services (as well as manufacturing abroad) guaranteed an adequate family income and the retention of agricultural capital and obviated the need to pay rent for urban housing.

The supply of non-manual labour is steadily increasing because industry and services can no longer provide jobs corresponding to scholastic attainments. The situation is rendered more difficult by an indeterminate element that is usually neglected by management and is becoming steadily more important, namely the "social" inelasticity of labour supply, or in other words the growing refusal on the part of the workers, particularly in the younger age groups, to engage in unskilled, monotonous, repetitive, alienating work, and their refusal of a technical and social division of work within the plant (scientific management) which no longer corresponds to the social characteristics of the labour supply. The accelerating spread of education stimulated by industrialisation is making existing modes of industrial production unacceptable: the employment of large numbers of workers at a level of skill which is below their potential achievement is tremendously wasteful and leads to increasing frustration among the increasingly educated labour force. Developments in industry since 1968 indicate that there has been a marked, profound qualitative change in the workers' attitude to their employment. Their refusal of the existing organisation of work, and their lack of consensus about it, seem to constitute a challenge to underlying elements of

Taylorism, namely not only fragmented and repetitive tasks but the division between the planning of work on the one hand and its passive execution by another subordinate class of workers.[5]

Thus the structure of the undertaking and the organisation of work were previously a technical matter of achieving an optimum combination among variables that were largely determined by technological characteristics; now they are becoming, in the eyes of both management and labour, and expression of a shifting balance of forces whereby technology is adapted to the requirements of the workforce.

The foregoing considerations explain how it comes about that in Italy changes in the organisation of work are mainly the result of trade union action and are reflected in collective agreements, often at the level of the undertaking.[6] The problem of work organisation is usually incidental to the issue of job classification and upgrading: management undertakes to change the organisation of work in acknowledgement of the workers' "right" to a continuing increase in their "professionalism", reflected in multi-skilling ("vocational mobility") which justifies wage increases. In other words arrangements are made to alter the traditional organisation of work by reducing the proportion of repetitive unskilled tasks, or even doing away with them altogether, in order to enable the workers to develop their qualifications and hence their earnings.

Already in 1970 an agreement for the ITALSIDER group provided for the introduction of a new job classification scheme for wage and salary earners on the basis of skill, together with innovations concerning job rotation and job content (enrichment). Again under the heading of "vocational mobility" a national agreement for the metal and mechanical engineering trades, signed in 1973, extended to the whole industry the principles of the ITALSIDER agreement, which were also embodied in agreements for other sectors of industry (e.g. chemicals) signed in the same year.

Numerous agreements along the same lines were then concluded for particular firms in the iron and steel industry (ITALSIDER, Dalmine,[7] Terni) and in mechanical engineering (e.g. Olivetti, Fiat). The Olivetti agreements of 1973 and 1974 made very detailed provision for the formation of an "integrated assembly unit" to carry out the entire assembly process, with particular attention to quality problems. This it was to do by—

(a) converting assembly work into the control and adjustment of a more mechanised production process;

(b) technical enrichment of individual tasks by a rearrangement that would transfer some maintenance functions to the group; and

(c) giving the group functional responsibilities such as quality control and inspection of raw material inputs.

A feature of all action taken in this field and all the agreements concluded has been the link between new forms of work organisation and the development of vocational skills, as is borne out by a paragraph of an important collective agreement (for the chemical industry) signed in April 1976:

Classification

The parties decide to look into possible changes in the existing grading structure, with reference to the particular technical and organisational realities in each sector, in order—

(a) to develop the workers' individual and collective skills and their participation in the production cycle, and to raise productivity by eliminating fragmented tasks and substituting coherent tasks, group work, work in the different stages of the production process, a reduction in the number of grades and training measures; and

(b) to develop a single grading system.[8]

The parties will also look into organisational changes (including their timing and implementation) that could help attain the objectives listed above and permit rapid structural adjustment to technological change in the industry.

In this context the parties may agree to introduce experimental innovations in work organisation and allocation so as to provide an agreed basis for the evaluation of such changes.

In short, the supply of industrial labour is inelastic and the workers are therefore in a strong bargaining position. The trade unions therefore aim to establish a more egalitarian system in factories by a collective upgrading, on the basis of length of service, of all workers relegated to unskilled work; and in response to trade union pressure in that direction an endeavour is made to introduce new forms of work organisation in order to make better use of the workers' potential.

Main new forms of work organisation

As shown earlier on in this paper, in Italy new forms of work organisation have been introduced on the initiative of the workers and the trade unions as a result of a change in the balance of forces between management and labour. The Government has taken no action directly affecting the organisation of work, whether by enacting legislation[9] or by setting up a specialised body, though in 1974 the Ministry of Labour commissioned ARPES, the research institute, to prepare a report on the organisation of work in factories.[10] On the other hand the major Italian industrial firms, besides engaging in a certain amount of research on the subject, are carrying out experiments and introducing changes. Special mention should be made of the Olivetti company, the IRI group (particularly on the iron and steel side), the ENI group (especially in petrochemicals) and Fiat. Though the means naturally differ, the goal is the same in each case: in view of the restrictions on the utilisation of labour, management aims at increased flexibility in the combination of the factors of production, which is essential if the production system is to remain efficient. In the following brief survey of changes introduced in Italy,[11] they will be classified in two groups according to whether more weight was attached to technological or organisational considerations.

Changes based primarily on technological considerations took place mainly in the mass production of machinery or machine parts (e.g. motors cars, household appliances, roller bearings) and were mainly directed at the elimination of dangerous, unhealthy or repetitive tasks through changes in layout or through mechanisation or automation.

The changes in the Fiat company covered all those aspects. For example, the layout of the new works at Cassino comprises four parallel and independent assembly lines, so that production can continue even when absenteeism is high. In addition, the job cycle of assembly workers has been prolonged from 1 to 4 minutes so as to reduce fragmentation of tasks; similar action has been taken in the plants at Termoli (the time spent working on a single engine has been increased to between 10 and 15 minutes) and Rivalta (dock assembly). The workers are thus much more free to allocate their time as they see fit and to work at their own pace, and have more opportunities of moving from one work station to another. At the Mirafiori works robots have been introduced to do all the welding, which was very trying work.

Much the same considerations prevailed upon the Zanussi (household appliances) firm: polymerisation in the manufacture of refrigerators, to which the workers objected as harmful work, was automated.

At the Airasca works of RIV-SKF (roller bearings) a technological improvement has allowed conversion to continuous flow production with integration of grinding, finishing, assembly and packing operations; there is automatic machine feed and automated transfer. The whole production process is controlled by groups of workers (usually three), who perform all production line functions, including quality control. In this particular case technological innovation has also allowed the workers' skills to be upgraded.

Other new forms of work organisation more specifically directed at upgrading skills have been introduced since the late 1960s. Mention should be made first of the Olivetti company. As already indicated, in the mid-1960s other Italian firms were trying to increase productivity through scientific management. The Olivetti company, however, developed a programme of research and experiments which highlighted the negative effects of fragmented tasks and identified opportunities for restructuring work. The firm's pragmatic and empirical approach was combined with an ongoing endeavour to establish principles and methods that would allow a constant spread of innovations. This activity led up to the constitution in the early 1970s of integrated assembly units each consisting of a group of workers responsible for attaining a number of objectives with an adequate allocation of resources. Within each unit, provision is made for a diversification of roles and tasks which makes the units independent of other subsystems in the plant. Each unit is engaged in the production of a specified product or component serving a recognisable purpose. These experiments had very satisfactory results: output reached very high levels in terms of quantity and especially quality; there was a marked fall in absenteeism, and the workforce as a whole became more skilled; and it became possible to adjust rapidly to innovations, especially in the electronics sector.

Similar experiments, in some 30 different shops, were made in the part of the iron and steel industry in which the Government has a stake (ITALSIDER, Dalmine, Terni): markedly more importance was attached to organisational than to technological considerations, and emphasis was placed on group decision-making and autonomy, which were admittedly to some extent dictated by the technical constraints of the production process. Under these new forms of work organisation, the power to take decisions concerning the regulation and control of the production process is redistributed through the integration of functions and operations within autonomous groups. In most cases these "work units" are given decision-making powers in the spheres of technology (starting-up and stopping of production), maintenance (dealing with breakdowns, periodic maintenance), management (weekly plan of operations, scheduling of holidays and rest periods, distribution of work among group members, supervision of implementation of the job rotation and upgrading scheme) and quality (quality control, product classification). This integration of functions and decisions involves a notable development of the workers' collective skills. It generally leads to a rise in productivity, and also has repercussions on the management structure of the factory: charge-hands are no longer needed and even the role of foremen calls for review and undergoes more or less extensive change, which sometimes gives rise to stress and strained relations within the factory.

ANIC (which belongs to the ENI state-owned group of firms) has also changed the organisation of work at its Ravenna petrochemical plant, and is now making the same changes in its other establishments. In this case too, a collective improvement in the workers' skills has been accompanied by the elimination of the post of charge hand and changes in the roles of foremen and functional services.

To sum up, it can be said that in view of economic and social developments, and in order to re-establish the degree of flexibility required to maintain productive efficiency, an endeavour has been made in Italy to discover an organisational model that overcomes social rigidity and allows some flexibility in the utilisation of manpower. In this search for efficiency, the new organisational models appear to be governed by the principles of the collective development of the skill of the workforce and control over the production process.[12]

The collective development of the skill of the workforce, achieved by an integration of skills and functions, constitutes an answer to the technical rigidity of the organisation since heightened individual and collective ability permits—

(a) more flexible utilisation of manpower;

(b) an improvement in output, both over time and in terms of quality; and

(c) fuller use of workers' vocational skills.

The second principle is control over the production process, i.e. the discretionary power of an individual worker or a group of workers to determine what rules should be followed in carrying out the operations required to maintain control over the production process. It is mainly through that principle that the new organisational models are intended to cope with the chief problem arising in the field of work organisation, namely the social rigidity of manpower. This control over the production process can be regarded as tantamount to an improvement in the quality of the work. When quality standards are raised, the workers acquire more power to determine not only the technical features of the application of the production process but also their own conditions of work.

The principles reflect the fact that as a result of changes in technology and in the workforce, the division of labour between manual and non-manual tasks is not the most efficient form of organisation of production in every case. Once the advantages of such a division of labour have been secured, further progress in improving productive efficiency calls for the reverse process of combination of functions. In other words, there comes a stage at which the mechanistic logic of the Taylorian model reduces efficiency because of the separation of functions and of unduly remote, high-level control over the factors that can produce as variety of unexpected breakdowns; and at that stage it becomes advantageous to integrate functions at the operative level. Increased efficiency is then sought not in a centralisation of decision-making but in the redistribution of decision-making powers according to the nature of the variables that have to be monitored. To put it differently, increased efficiency is then achieved not by increasing the productivity of the individual manual worker but by reducing the horizontal and vertical division of labour.

CASE STUDY

The Dalmine tube mill at Apuania

Under a quality improvement and product diversification programme, the Dalmine company decided in 1972 to instal new tempering, sizing, straightening and finishing equipment in its tube mill at Apuania. The new equipment comprises technologically very advanced machinery, hitherto never used in Italy, and takes the place of an old heat treatment shop of a very rudimentary character. The management decided that this innovation should be accompanied by a new form of work organisation directed at achieving a high level of efficiency by optimalising the combination of technological and human or social variables.

Initial situation

Dalmine is a limited company, most of the shares being in the hands of the state-owned IRI[13] group. Among the iron and steel firms in which the State has an interest, Dalmine specialises in the manufacture of steel tubes. With an output of about a million tons a year, it holds between 35 and 40 per cent of the home market, being the largest such firm in Italy and exporting about a quarter of what it produces. Although it produces the entire range of steel tubes, it has for some years concentrated on quality products, especially for petroleum research and extraction. The firm has six works—two in the north of Italy (Dalmine, Costa Volpino), two in the centre (Apuania, Piombino) and two in the south (Taranto, Torre Annunziata). The head office in Milan has a functional management structure, with separate divisions for production, marketing, administration and finance, and personnel. The firm employs about 14,000 people, of whom about 11,400 are wage earners and 2,600 salaried employees and supervisory staff.

The Apuania mill specialises in the manufacture of quality tubes for the boring of oil wells and the extraction of the oil. It, too, has a functional management structure, with divisions for programming, time and methods study, quality control, maintenance, administration, personnel and production. Each year the mill produces about 150,000 tonnes of quality tubes, of which about 130,000 go through the rectification process. The raw materials (ingots and billets) are converted into some 40 different types of tubes, which are despatched directly from the works to the customer. The equipment has been continually modernised in conformity with the latest developments in the technology of iron and steel fabrication, and has been valued at US$40,000 per worker.

The human factor none the less still plays an important part in the total production process. There are about 1,500 wage earners, 250 salaried employees and supervisors and five senior managers at the works. Over the past few years the workforce has increased slightly, owing in particular to a reduction (brought about by collective bargaining) in hours of work, which stood at the time of writing at 39 a week. The skill of the workforce is average, and the level of general education is rising quite fast. Labour turnover is negligible, while the rate of absenteeism corresponds roughly to the industrial average. The workforce is highly unionised, and much given to bargaining, but labour disputes remain within reasonable bounds in accordance with the national trend in the metallurgical industries (the management shows great readiness to bargain with the unions). At regular intervals the workers elect shop stewards, who sit on the works council along with local trade union officers.

Over the past few years, collective bargaining at the level of the undertaking has been concerned in particular with job classification, the workers' aim being to achieve collective upgrading on the basis of length of service. Another subject of discussion has been the internal mobility of labour in view of the strong decline in the possibility of transferring personnel from one job to another. These developments have gradually led to a further diminution in the degree of flexibility of labour utilisation.

The job classification scheme established by collective agreements covers wage earners, salaried employees and supervisors. There are eight grades: I to V comprise both wage and salary earners, while VI to VIII consist exclusively of salaried employees and supervisory staff. About 80 per cent of the wage earners employed by the firm as a whole are in grades IV and V, which correspond to quite a high degree of skill. This distribution is due partly to the nature of the work required (modern plant and complex metallurgical processes) and partly to trade union pressure for the collective upgrading of workers formerly in the lower grades.

The Dalmine company reacted to the trade union pressure which was bringing about a general upgrading and increase in remuneration, and to the change in the composition of the workforce (longer schooling, incorporation in industrial society) which gave it a margin of unused potential. The firm's policy has been to adjust production and the organisation of work in such a way as to promote vocational development and a better utilisation of the workers' potential. This is to be achieved by granting the workers more freedom and responsibility, concentrating on results in terms of the over-all efficiency of the undertaking, and giving practical recognition to the role played by each individual. The firm's approach to the problems of organisation thus corresponds to the general tendency that has emerged in Italy in this respect, as a result of trade union pressure and of the research carried out in the early 1970s, particularly within the IRI group to which Dalmine belongs. New forms of work organisation have thus been gradually introduced in different workshops since 1973 with a view to the gradual improvement of the workers' skills, of functional relations within each factory and of restructuring methods.

Introduction of a new form of work organisation

For the new form of work organisation to be introduced at the Apuania mill, a working party was set up consisting of experts from the personnel, time and methods study, quality control and production divisions of the general and works managements. The working party carried out a preliminary analysis of the situation and agreed on a methodology. It was then enlarged by the addition of workers' representatives nominated by the works council. In view of the working party's advisory functions, these representatives joined in the planning of the project as experts, leaving the works management and the local trade union branches entirely free to negotiate on the choice among the alternative proposals the working party would make. The workers also played an active part in the working party's activities through interviews and discussions concerning the manufacturing process.

The working party held its first meetings when the new equipment was undergoing its trial run. The shop as a whole was divided into a number of areas each physically distinct and devoted to operations having an ascertainable result and including inspection functions. The analysis covered heat treatment; sizing; straightening; Magnatest I inspection; ultrasonic inspection; magnetisation, surface inspection and grinding; cutting to length; and functional relations with the programming, quality control and maintenance departments. About 30 work posts and 150 workers (on shifts) were involved.

Once the analysis was completed various possible forms of organisation were worked out. The working party's final proposals embodied alternative forms of semi-autonomous group working, one based on stages in the production process and the other on homogeneity of functions. Under both alternatives quality control and day-to-day maintenance would be assigned to the groups while production planning would be left to the planning department and the shop foreman.

Under the arrangement ultimately adopted, there are four groups, each corresponding to a stage of the production process, as follows: heat treatment; sizing and straightening; quality control and grinding; cutting to length. Each group is multi-skilled, every member being available to perform any of the functions assigned to the group. The arrangement had been negotiated with the trade unions, and a works agreement of April 1975 provided that after the initial phase each group would be qualified for inclusion in class V. A new entrant would be given 21 months to become fully multi-skilled; theoretical and practical training would be available after working hours.

Group A (seven workers at any one time, out of a total of 37 for 16 shift periods a week) carries out all the tasks involved in the efficient operation of the heat treatment equipment. It has sole responsibility for taking delivery of the raw material, stock control in that respect, the feeding and operation of the machinery (in accordance with standard operating procedure), maintenance of the electrical and electronic systems, keeping the records required for production control purposes, and arranging job rotation within the group and all scheduled rest periods (including holidays). Group B (four workers at any one time, out of a total of 18) sets, adjusts and maintains the sizing and straightening machines, and arranges job rotation and scheduled rest periods. Group C (11 workers at any one time, out of 51) is in charge of non-destructive testing by electromagnetic and ultrasonic means. It sets and adjusts the necessary equipment, makes the sampling arrangements and carries out the grinding operations required; it maintains a detailed record of flaws, and arranges job rotation within the group and scheduled rest periods. Group D (also 11 workers at any one time out of a total of 51) is in charge of cutting, trimming and blunting, size control, and the stocking and despatch of the tubes. Like the other groups, this one also adjusts and maintains the necessary machinery and arranges job rotation and scheduled rest periods.

On each shift the work of the groups is co-ordinated by a foreman, who is also responsible for liaison with the functional departments (e.g. production planning, metallurgical standards), suggesting improvements to the equipment and checking attainment of quantity and quality targets. He also takes any necessary steps to facilitate the work of the groups.

Results

An initial assessment of results after the first 18 months is as follows. From the technical and economic points of view it is noted that the equipment, which was expensive and of an entirely novel kind for the Dalmine company, reached the required level of performance very quickly and without any major difficulty. This result is attributed to the new form of work organisation, particularly the thorough integration of work preparation and operations with the adjustment and servicing of equipment within each group. Output and reject rates are also satisfactory.

As regards the effects on the workforce it should be borne in mind that 70 per cent of the workers concerned came from another shop within the Apuania works; their age, length of service and skill were about average. Most of them were production workers, and it had been decided not to put maintenance workers on the project because their specialised background might have led to a re-emergence of a technical division of labour which would have been a hindrance to collective group working. In fact skills have been very evenly developed, and it can be said that each group rapidly became multi-skilled. Initial resistance to job rotation was overcome as a result of the gradual growth in each group of social pressure which caused individual group members to be very assiduous in attendance at vocational training courses. The same social pressure and group consciousness led to a marked fall in absenteeism; in other words, multi-skilling led to group consciousness, with favourable results in terms of productivity.

On the other hand this behavioural change also had negative results. Extreme mobility within the groups is a remarkable advantage in view of the growing lack of flexibility in other shops, but the mobility is offset by some reserve in dealings with outsiders: each group is now somewhat reserved in its relations with other groups, the foremen and the functional departments. The immediate negative repercussions on the foreman's role can be remedied only by giving the groups collective co-ordination duties in relation to the shop as a whole. At the moment such a change is ruled out for technological and vocational training reasons, but there is no other way of enabling the new form of work organisation to develop.

Notes

[1] See in particular Istituto Gramsci: *Scienza e organizzazione del lavoro,* Atti del convegno tenuto a Torino l'8-9-10 giugno 1973, edited by Franco Ferri (Rome, Editori Riuniti, 1973, 2 vols.).

[2] This part of the paper is based on various documents of ARPES, which is an institute of applied research concerning economic and social plans. In 1970 the IRI group of undertakings commissioned the institute to carry out a research project concerning *(a)* major innovations with regard to work organisation, *(b)* the labour market, and *(c)* the establishment of a methodology for analysis and innovation in respect of work organisation, as a basis for current action in the IRI group. The results of *(a)* and *(b)* have been published in *Tecnologia, sistemi organizzativi, qualificazione,* Ricerca INTERSIND-ARPES (Rome, Anonima Tipografica Editrice Laziale, 1973), Vol. 1: *Esperienze innovative in Europa,* and Vol. 2: *Mercato del lavoro e qualificazione professionale.* Point *(c)* involved research in undertakings engaged in three different types of production. In 1974 the institute was also commissioned by the Minister of Labour to prepare a report on the organisation of manual work in Italian industry—see *L'organizzazione del lavoro operaio in fabbrica,* Rapporto conclusivo di una ricerca svolta dall'ARPES su incarico del Ministero del Lavoro, published as No. 9, Nov. 1974, of *Quaderni di formazione ISFOL* (Rome, Istituto per lo sviluppo della formazione professionale dei lavoratori).

[3] The correctness of this interpretation (taken from *Mercato del lavoro e qualificazione professionale,* op. cit., pp. 25-32) has been fully confirmed by labour market movements over the past few years.

[4] ibid., pp. 10, 66. The report suggests (ibid., p. 31) that a reader interested in this casual labour market might also wish to look up Paolo Sylos-Labini: "Precarious employment in Sicily", in *International Labour Review,* Mar. 1964, pp. 268-285.

[5] *Mercato del lavoro e qualificazione professionale,* op. cit., pp. 7, 11-12.

[6] See Matteo Rollier: "The organisation of work and industrial relations in the Italian engineering industry", in *Labour and Society,* Apr. 1976.

[7] See below, pp. 72-76.

[8] Covering manual workers, office workers, supervisors, technicians and middle management.

[9] The so-called "Workers' Charter" (Act No. 300, to make provisions respecting the protection of workers' freedom and dignity, trade union freedom and freedom of action within the workplace, and provisions respecting placement, published in ILO: *Legislative Series,* 1970—It. 2) sets bounds on the use of factory labour but has no direct bearing on the organisation of work.

[10] See note 2 above.

[11] This survey is derived from recent research on the part of INTERSIND: see C. Sampietro (ed.): *Nuove vie della organizzazione del lavoro: Esperienze e prospettive* (ISEDI, 1976).

[12] This analysis is derived from ARPES publications.

[13] Istituto per la Ricostruzione Industriale.

USSR

Sign used in the tables · = zero

USSR

A. S. Dovba, Y. L. Shagalov, I. I. Shapiro and A. F. Zubkova*

NATIONAL CONDITIONS

A major factor in the expansion of the economy and the social development of the USSR is the scientific organisation of work with the aim of ensuring the most effective and harmonious combination of human energies and new technologies in the production process.

Origins and foundations of the scientific organisation of work in the USSR

Since it first came into existence the Soviet State has devoted special attention to the question of improving the organisation of work on the basis of scientific achievements and innovations. At that period in history the work of Frederick W. Taylor and his followers in the field of work organisation, aptly described as efficiency engineering, had been widely recognised and applied in the industrialised countries of the West. Work organisation established on the basis of Taylorite principles initially ensured a substantial reduction in the cost of production and an increase in profits.

In the early years of Soviet industrialisation the advocates of the scientific organisation of work rejected Taylorism, considering Taylor's methods exploitative and alien to the ideals of a socialist state. This rejection was based on the following evaluation of Taylorism: its methods of research and recommendations are unsound from the point of view of human physiology and psychology; it strives after excessive fragmentation of jobs without regard to the effects this has on a person's health and the development of society; it negates the creative character of human work; it regards human work as an aggregate of mechanical movements without regard to their connection with modern tools; and it limits the scope for the adoption of more efficient working methods by the individual worker without regard to his inter-relationship with the collective work process. They argued that in the USSR, by contrast, measures aimed at improving work organisation should take fully into account the changes which the scientific and technological revolution and the social development of society had brought in the character and content of human labour.

---

* Labour Research Institute, State Committee on Labour and Social Questions, USSR Council of Ministers. See also footnote on p. 101.

Technological advances have led to a steady increase in the technical equipment of factories. Consequently, the ratio of human to mechanical work in the total expenditure on production has changed in favour of the machine. Profound qualitative changes have also occurred as a result of the switch from manual to mechanised work and to comprehensive mechanisation and automation of the production processes. These changes do not diminish the human role; they actually accentuate its importance: as the level of technical equipment rises the work done by people becomes even more complex and crucial. The introduction of universal secondary education has significantly raised the educational level of the workers. For example, the proportion of workers with secondary and higher education increased from 65.3 per cent in 1970 to 76.7 per cent in 1976. As the educational and cultural level of the population rises, the workers look for more interest in their jobs and more possibilities for constant creative development at work. In these circumstances the role of the scientific organisation of work in increasing both productive efficiency and social development gains enormously in importance.

The improvement of work organisation at different stages in the history of the USSR was determined by the level of development of the productive forces. In the first years of the existence of the Soviet Union, when a considerable proportion of industrial undertakings employed manual labour, priority was given to determining the proper working methods and the mass training to be given to the workers. The efforts of physiologists at that time were directed mainly towards determining the permissible physical loads for the worker in the work process. At that time dozens of special laboratories and institutes were set up to conduct various types of research in the field of work organisation.

The work of the Central Labour Institute in this respect was particularly effective. Work methods and training systems developed by the Institute were widely used in the training of workers and foremen in all branches of industry. The Central Labour Institute ran 1,700 training centres, employed more than 20,000 instructors and trained more than 500,000 skilled workers for industrial undertakings. The Institute's methods were used by almost all undertakings in the country for the training of their own workers and foremen.

Spread of automation

In more recent years the increasing industrialisation of the national economy has been reflected in extensive mechanisation and automation. At this stage the problems of developing collective forms of work organisation became more pressing, and attention was concentrated on multi-machine operation, multi-skill development, optimum methods of servicing modern equipment, drawing up work and rest schedules achieving the best possible balance between expenditure of muscular and nervous energy and making work more interesting and attractive. The accent then shifted from individual work stations to the organisation of work at the level of the workshop or undertaking. Thus the scientific organisation of work became more closely linked with improved production techniques and increased efficiency. These trends are now predominant in all branches of the Soviet economy.

An analysis of changes in job content resulting from automation shows that this process is not identical at all stages. Partial automation of production processes, which consists in automating isolated operations in the running of a machine before a transition is made to semi-automatic and automatic machines, eliminates some of the cyclically recurring elements from the content of the work process and simplifies the work directly involved. At the same time, however, there is an increase in the amount of work involved in adjusting, resetting and maintaining equipment and machinery.

The establishment of automated lines and other mechanical systems for full automation of the production process means major changes in the economics of production and the nature and content of the workers' jobs. As a result of comprehensive automation of production, control, transport and storage operations, labour productivity becomes between three and five times greater than with non-automated production lines. In the USSR more than half of the over-all increase in labour productivity can be attributed to the introduction of new instruments of work and the improvement of production technology in industry. It is estimated that during the current tenth (1976-80) five-year plan about 90 per cent of the growth in industrial production will be achieved through an increase in labour productivity. The principal means of increasing labour productivity are all-round mechanisation and automation of production processes, increases in the power available per worker, improvements in the organisation of work, production and management and improvements in the workers' skills to match the demands of scientific and technological progress.

As automation proceeds, labour expenditure in general is reduced and redistributed: there is a sharp reduction in the labour expended on carrying out the simple mechanical movements connected with loading and driving the equipment and there is an increase in the labour expended on supervising the functioning of the equipment, its adjustment and its maintenance in working condition. The resulting increase in the complexity and degree of interest of work on automated lines and the new and higher skills required of the workers are matched by steadily rising levels of general education.

On the economic plane, automation significantly changes the correlation between the expenditure of human and mechanical energy in favour of the machine. In industry in general amortisation costs are equivalent to about 40 per cent of the total wage bill (including social insurance allocations). In the majority of automated lines the reverse is found: amortisation costs are greater than the wage bill. Therefore, the effectiveness of the scientific organisation of work on automated lines depends substantially on ensuring uninterrupted operation of the automated equipment.

The prevalence of complex work in automated production makes it necessary for new ways to be found to improve work methods. It is of decisive importance in this connection to work out the best methods of monitoring mechanical operations, detecting defects quickly, and finding and eliminating their causes as rapidly as possible. A successful application of this policy has been made at the First State Bearings Factory, where labour productivity among the adjusters on automated lines has increased by between 30 and 50 per cent thanks to the adoption of improved methods of adjusting the equipment and monitoring its operation.

On the organisational plane, a characteristic feature of automated production is the close interdependence between the individual links of the automated line. In these conditions the most effective form of organisation is the combined work brigade made up of workers with different skills. The work of the members of these brigades is evaluated according to the final output of the automated line.

Efforts to improve work organisation in the Soviet Union take into account the level of automation and its effects on job content. In spite of the emphasis placed on the long-term problems of work organisation connected with comprehensive mechanisation and automation, every precaution is taken to ensure that the need to make work more interesting and to improve conditions of work in undertakings where automation is not yet complete will not be overlooked.

Implications for the workers

The planned mechanisation and automation of production processes are closely integrated with the allocation and redeployment of manpower, and do not result in unemployment. However, automation alters the content of work, mainly through the elimination of monotonous mechanical movements and by making the work more interesting and attractive. It also calls for a higher level of education and skill. The need to provide industry with highly skilled workers is mainly met through the existing systems of general and specialised education and through training and upgrading of workers at all levels. The training of production workers is centrally organised by the State, in vocational and technical schools. These schools prepare for the national economy generally educated, technically trained and thoroughly responsible young workers, competent in their respective trades, and capable of meeting the requirements of present-day production and of its prospective development.

In connection with automation, the scientific organisation of work facilitates the efficient utilisation of equipment and working time, the provision of opportunities for the workers to make practical use of their general and vocational education, the all-round creative development of the workers, the establishment of favourable working conditions in undertakings, and the instilling in the workers of a spirit of discipline, comradeship, mutual aid and collectivism that will help to mould a new man. Since their interests are so directly involved in achieving these objectives, the workers take an active part in the development and introduction of new forms of work organisation.

The reduction of the amount of manual, low-skilled and physically arduous work through mechanisation and automation also helps to reduce the incidence of diseases and accidents (and that in turn is an important factor in improving the utilisation of equipment and other production resources).

Objectives and methods of work organisation

In June 1967 an all-Union conference on work organisation in industry and construction was held in the USSR. The conference was attended by workers at all levels, engineering and technical staff, research personnel and government officials. After reviewing expert summaries and analyses of the experiments carried out, the conference defined the content and basic objectives of the scientific organisation of work. The conference indicated that in current conditions work organisation could be regarded as scientific when it was based on the systematic introduction of the achievements of science and progressive methods into the undertaking, when it produced the best possible combination of technology and human effort in a single production process, when it secured the optimum increase in labour productivity and when it contributed to the workers' health and the progressive transformation of work itself into the most meaningful activity in man's daily life.

From this definition emerge the three major functions of the scientific organisation of work at the present time:

(1) It must actively contribute to the economic development of the country. By combining technology and people in a single production process in the best possible way, it is called upon to ensure the most effective use of labour and material resources and a steady increase in labour productivity.

(2) The scientific organisation of work has a major role to play in creating favourable working conditions and protecting the health of the people, who are the main productive force of society.

(3) Finally, it has the extremely important function of achieving one of the basic aims of the social development of Soviet society, namely educating the new man in the work process and transforming work itself into the most meaningful human activity.

The three functions described above underlie the main specific objectives of the scientific organisation of work at the present time, namely—

(a) developing new and efficient forms of division of labour and labour co-operation;

(b) improving the organisation and servicing of workplaces;

(c) studying and disseminating advanced methods of work;

(d) training and upgrading of personnel;

(e) improving the methods of fixing work norms;

(f) improving conditions of work in every possible way so as to make them less arduous and healthier; and

(g) fostering among manual and non-manual workers a conscientious attitude towards work and the strictest observance of public and labour discipline.

The scientific organisation of work is not a static concept. It is constantly being improved to reflect the latest developments and achievements and the most advanced production methods. A characteristic feature at present is the wider use being made of the findings of research specifically aimed at improving work organisation. The scientific organisation of work draws on the methods and results of research in various fields of knowledge and applies them to the complex and varied processes of human labour.

The technical sciences provide the foundation for determining the best possible choices for selection and installation of industrial equipment, for mechanising the work process and selecting the organisation structure. Biological sciences establish the basis for ascertaining the most favourable mental and physical conditions of work for the human organism so as to ensure high levels of efficiency and long, active working lives. The social sciences provide correlations between new forms of work organisation and the development of smoothly functioning team work, public participation in improving work organisation, the establishment of work standards, moral incentives to work, and heightening the attractiveness of work itself and stimulating the conscientiousness of the workers. Educational research is used in selecting the most efficient forms and methods of training and upgrading and in carrying out vocational and skill training of the workers. Economics provides the basis for determining the most efficient methods of work for individuals or groups of workers, the correlation between the workers of various categories and the labour costs, and the proportions of expenditure to be devoted to human and mechanical work. Economics makes it possible to evaluate and compare the standards of work organisation both in single plants and throughout whole branches of industry, and to determine the effectiveness of new forms of work organisation and various forms of material incentives.

Research in all these fields is used in solving the problems involved in adapting machines and other equipment to man, and more generally in the interaction between the worker and the instruments of production. On the practical plane this means, first, that wide use is made in work organisation schemes of the mechanisation of highly labour-intensive manual jobs, the improvement of working conditions, the development of multi-machine operation, and the mechanisation and automation of engineering and accounting activities. Secondly, new forms of work organisation aim at improving the organisation and management of production and ensuring the most effective co-ordination of people and techniques within production groups. Thirdly, the requirements of new forms of work organisation must be taken into account in machine and plant design.

Principles currently applied

In adopting this approach to the organisation of the work process the following principles are applied.

Optimal content and structure of the work process. The work process must ensure the most favourable combination of mental and physical activity for the workers, an even loading of the various organs and a suitable pace of work, and a synchronisation of human and mechanical activities involved. The physical and nervous loads must not exceed the optimum values established on the basis of psycho-physiological studies.

Parallelism. The work of man and machine and the work of several machines must be synchronised.

Economy of muscular and nervous energy. Unnecessary and exhausting working methods, operations and movements are to be eliminated.

Continuity. Each succeeding part of the work process should be the natural continuation of preceding ones.

Planned and anticipatory servicing of workplaces. Basic and auxiliary operations should be synchronised, and a strict schedule set up for their performance. Observance of this principle makes it possible to cut down the losses of working time that arise in particular when equipment and workplaces are serviced during scheduled breaks or between shifts; it makes it possible to service workplaces wholly or predominantly without stopping the machinery and wasting the time of production workers.

Motion study. A favourable posture and suitable trajectory for their movements have to be chosen for the workers on the basis of the laws of physiology, as applicable to work. When choosing a posture for the worker account is taken of the fact that the muscular tension required when work is performed standing up will be 15 per cent higher than if the work is done in a sitting position; in a bent-over position the tension is twice that observed in a sitting position. Alternating standing and sitting considerably lowers fatigue, since in this case the load falls alternately on different muscles. Therefore there is a tendency to enable the workers to change their posture freely by working alternately sitting and standing. Co-ordination of the worker's hands with the controls should be steady; an easy grip is thus provided, with proper application and distribution of effort. When selecting the most appropriate movements for the worker, preference is given to symmetrical movements over non-symmetrical ones; also to flowing and uninterrupted movements over jagged ones, and to circular ones over those proceeding along straight lines. The lifting of components and other objects is avoided.

Vocational aptitude. Psychological, physiological, educational and training characteristics should make workers particularly fit for a task of a given nature and content. This can be ensured by means of vocational selection, formal training and upgrading and on-the-job training, which lead up to the acquisition by the worker of the necessary qualifications and productive habits, and soon to familiarity with efficient working methods. In the plant workers should be assigned to the work that promotes the best possible use of their education and skills.

Optimum utilisation of equipment and tools. Schedules based on technical and economic research are drawn up which reduce to a minimum the total expenditure of human labour and resources, both on individual operations and on the production process as a whole.

Optimal combinations of work and rest for production workers. This principle governs the beginning and the end of work periods, the succession of shifts, and the start and finish of meal periods and other scheduled breaks within shifts, thus ensuring a regular alternation of work and rest, avoiding excessive fatigue for the worker and allowing the timely completion of such activities as repairs, loading and other preparations, including the fastening on of equipment.

Observance of these principles is one of the main prerequisites for high productivity and favourable working conditions. The application of many of them is determined by the nature of the equipment, and by technical and organisational requirements. For the most part, however, it depends on the workers' methods of working. Such methods are gradually improved as new skills are acquired.

Planning and introduction of new forms of work organisation

In the USSR the introduction of new forms of work organisation is based on joint participation of the State and trade unions, the management of undertakings and the workers involved, and on state planning combined with wide initiative on the part of the production groups of the undertakings and workshops and even of the individual workers.

Scientific achievements and advanced production methods are combined into new work forms and all-round improvements are sought in respect of organisation, standard-setting, and material and moral incentives for the worker.

The undertakings' work organisation and planning activities are carried out by a unit corresponding to the size and type of production, for example the department of work organisation and wages, the work organisation laboratory or some appropriate bureaux or groups. Such bodies carry out organisational, research and practical work in this field.

Having a direct interest in the positive outcome of measures to improve work organisation, the workers take an active part in these activities. The most widespread form of worker participation in the introduction of new forms of work organisation is through the constitution of teams composed of workers and of experts such as engineers, economists, organisation specialists and physiologists. Not infrequently, in fact, teams like these are set up on the workers' own initiative. The remarkable effectiveness of the work organisation teams can be ascribed to the fact that the right of workers and specialists to take initiatives is a guarantee of the soundness of the work organisation measures adopted and their effective implementation on the shop floor.

Councils of local organisations of scientific and technical societies and the All-Union Society of Inventors and Efficiency Experts, public economic analysis offices, public standard-fixing bureaux and other organisations in which the workers are active play an important role in bringing to light an undertaking's potential, particularly as regards the efficient use of working time, equipment and tools. The proposals put forward by these bodies are given preliminary consideration and are analysed by ad hoc public committees and subsequently by the workers' assemblies of the workshops concerned.

The work organisation proposals and measures subsequently adopted, after thorough discussion by management and the trade union committee of the enterprise, are incorporated into appropriate plans for production sections and workshops.

As already mentioned the Soviet trade unions, which now have more than 107 million members, play a major role in the development and introduction of the scientific organisation of work. The unions are actively engaged in improving conditions of work for both manual and non-manual workers and in developing a conscientious, active and creative attitude to work. Each year the workers put forward more than 5 million proposals, a considerable number of which are aimed at improving work organisation. Socialist emulation and other ways of improving the workers' productivity are given every possible encouragement. Among the obligations of individuals and groups of workers, great importance is attached to measures aimed at improving work organisation. The most important of these measures are included in the plant or enterprise collective agreements, and their implementation is supervised by trade union committees.

In the drawing up of individual work organisation plans, great importance is attached to making the work more interesting, to improving working conditions and to the development of the workers involved. Parallel with these plans, more general schemes for improvement of staff conditions have been widely adopted in recent years. Such schemes provide for progressive changes in the skill structure of the staff, the raising of the educational and cultural standards of the workers, the improvement of their housing and day-to-day living conditions and the fostering of a communist attitude to work.

Plans for the social development of the staff are drawn up by the management of the undertaking together with the social organisations and creative workers' units. The draft plans are fully discussed at the workers' assemblies and production meetings. At the present time more than 50,000 undertakings and organisations operate social development plans.

National planning of the scientific organisation of work in all branches of industrial production is carried out by a special section of the State Planning Committee (Introduction of Scientific Work Organisation Section), which defines the tasks of the ministries, departments and councils of ministers of the all-Union republics in these matters. The national economic plan firmly establishes the most important and effective measures to be adopted in all branches of the national economy. These measures include the following:

(a) models for the organisation of work stations for the more common trades, for engineers and other technical staff and for non-manual workers;

(b) norms and standards setting output rates for workers, engineers and other technical staff and non-manual workers in the economy as a whole and for particular branches of it;

(c) model plans for the organisation of work units within a workshop;

(d) organisation charts of new forms of work structure;

(e) the introduction of multi-machine operation;

(f) multi-skilling; and

(g) the introduction of forms of organisation adapted to group production.

Current and long-term plans of the various Soviet republics for the introduction of important measures in the field of work organisation are approved by the State Planning Committee of the USSR and the State Committee on Labour and Social Questions with the participation of the All-Union Central Council of Trade Unions. The State Committee of the USSR Council of Ministers on Labour and Social Questions is responsible for co-ordinating the activities of the ministries and departments as regards work organisation and the management of production. The work in this field is carried out by the Department of Labour Productivity, Organisation and Standard Setting, the Department of Working

Conditions and the various departments for the different sectors of industry, in close contact with other appropriate organisations.

The ministries responsible for keeping an eye on progress in this field in the various branches of industry play an important role both in introducing new forms of work organisation and in lending practical assistance. Within the ministries, expert guidance is provided by special units dealing with work organisation, wages and personnel.

The USSR's system of planning and supervision is directed not only at improving the economic results achieved by an undertaking but also at the over-all solution of such important social problems as making work more interesting and improving working conditions. Economic efficiency is assessed by a common method approved by the State Labour Committee of the USSR, which ensures reliability and comparability of all the calculations utilised. The USSR's statistics on the scientific organisation of work provide a basis for guiding and supervising the introdcution of new forms of work organisation in the undertakings, for detailed analysis and evaluation of the progress achieved and its effectiveness, and for the drawing up and soundness of current and long-term plans.

The country's main scientific establishment for co-ordinating the activities of the research institutes and design organisations of the ministries and departments of labour is the Labour Research Institute, which assists undertakings and organisations in the practical adaptation and application of research findings.

Specialised organisations—centres established in many branches of industry—ensure co-ordination and, relying on the findings of current research, provide practical assistance to different industrial undertakings for introducing new forms of work organisation. The branch centres carry out their activities under the guidance of the All-Union Scientific Methods Centre for the Organisation of Labour and the Management of Production of the State Committee of the USSR Council of Ministers on Labour and Social Questions, using the methods and standards developed by the Labour Research Institute. Relations between the centres and the undertakings are based mainly on self-financing agreements. At the present time there are more than 140 scientific work organisation centres operating in industry.

Work methods study in the USSR is based on wide-scale theoretical and practical research in the fields of political economy, labour economics, labour physiology and psychology, and industrial design. Research in these fields is carried out and co-ordinated not only by the Labour Research Institute but also by such bodies as the Institutes of Economics of the USSR Academy of Sciences and the academies of the Union republics, the Institute of Labour Hygiene and Occupational Diseases of the USSR Academy of Medical Sciences and the All-Union Scientific Research Institute for Aesthetic Styling in Engineering.

Standards and work organisation models

Standards and work organisation models, the development and introduction of which have considerably expanded in recent years, play a major role in the over-all system for the improvement of work organisation. They convert research findings into forms suitable for introduction at the level of the undertaking either directly or with slight adjustments to suit the conditions in a given undertaking, workshop or workplace. In this way they form connecting links between science and production. Their use eliminates duplication of design work by undertakings and allows the staff of the undertakings' work organisation sections to make fuller use of the achievements of science and advanced production methods.

To determine production norms in industry in the USSR the technological and work processes are broken down into their constituent parts, which are then analysed. The best means of attaining the objective is then outlined and a time schedule is drawn up for the performance of the component parts of the entire process. Standards set by this analytical method and directed towards the attainment of maximum efficiency in terms of working time and equipment are called "technically founded". This technical foundation is a basic aspect of the justification of labour standards, but it is not the only one. In fact technically founded norms are not based solely on technological criteria but also on economic, physiological, psychological and sociological factors. However, the technical justification of labour standards is a prerequisite for the most efficient use of equipment, tools and plant. Their economic justification enables valid comparisons to be made between and among enterprises and their production results, since the organisation and operations of all enterprises follow similar labour standards or norms. At the moment four types of work organisation standards are being developed, for *(a)* design equipment, technological processes and undertakings, *(b)* work organisation, *(c)* working conditions, and *(d)* labour expenditure.

Work organisation models designed for standard workplaces, production departments and workshops incorporate the best possible solutions for all aspects of work organisation. These models are produced by industrial branch research institutes, design organisations and work organisation centres utilising the findings of scientific research and progressive methods. The undertakings make use of the models in planning and introducing new forms of work organisation.

Current aims

The current five-year plan attaches major importance to the solution of problems in the field of labour, which is the main area of man's daily activities, and to the formation and development of his personality. The plan provides, in particular, for the improvement of conditions of work, the heightening of its creative character, all possible reductions in unduly arduous physical labour, the raising of the workers' standards of general and technical education, the improvement of medical services, the extension of the period of economic activity within the human life span and the development of the workers' participation in public affairs.

In view of the advantages that result from full mechanisation and automation of production, the main aim in the development of production in the USSR is to set up automated lines, departments and workshops. Between 1965 and 1975 the number of automated lines and mechanised and automated sections, workshops, plants and undertakings in Soviet industry trebled. The current five-year plan provides for a rapid increase in the output of numerically controlled machines, a considerable rise in the output of automated production lines, the organisation of fully automated but easily readjustable production lines, and the setting up of complexes of highly productive equipment that can be run with the help of electronic computers which can be introduced into industrial workshops engaged in mass or batch production. In undertakings where these ultra-modern methods of production are being introduced, intensive work such as assembling, loading and unloading has already been fully mechanised and automated.

CASE STUDIES

Industry in the USSR has acquired extensive experience in improving work organisation. Study of this experience shows that undertakings have adopted different approaches using the most varied methods and means.

Development of division of labour and labour co-operation in a number of industrial undertakings

The division of labour and labour co-operation are being developed in quite a number of industrial undertakings in the USSR with a view to ensuring high levels of productivity, the efficient use of equipment and the most favourable combination of physical and mental work.

Functional and technological division of labour

In the Soviet Union a distinction is drawn between the functional division of labour on the one hand and, on the other, the technological division of labour whereby the content of each technological operation performed by a worker is defined.

Attention is first of all devoted to a functional division of labour in the production process between production workers and auxiliaries. If production workers can be freed from tasks such as carrying materials, half-finished products, instruments and other equipment to their workplaces or sharpening tools, and if those duties can be transferred to auxiliary workers, essential tasks can be mechanised and better organised and fuller use can be made of working time and of plant. However, a complete separation of auxiliary from primary functions might make the work less interesting. Therefore many undertakings engaged in mass production give their machine operators some adjusting functions to perform as well, and it is found that as a result their work becomes more interesting, the use of working time is frequently improved and favourable conditions are established for the workers' development.

The functional division of labour is very closely bound up with the organisation of production. The separation of auxiliary from primary or production functions facilitates the organisation of well equipped specialised sub-units responsible for such tasks as repairs, the transport and storage of materials and semi-finished products, and housekeeping. In particular, improved functional division of labour involves regulation of the work of maintenance personnel. This can lead to improved utilisation of the working time of production workers and of the equipment, with fewer maintenance personnel and a more economical maintenance system, thereby increasing production efficiency. In this respect it is interesting to note the experience of the "Fiftieth Anniversary of the USSR" Volga automobile works and a number of other undertakings where all the functions connected with the maintenance of essential production equipment throughout the enterprise are entrusted to specialised sub-units located in selected major production departments of the factory. Such a system enables auxiliary work to be more fully mechanised, arduous manual work eliminated and more extensive use made of the working time of the maintenance personnel.

As regards mechanised and conveyor lines, the most important and complex problems are those of reducing monotony, making the work more interesting and eliminating the unfavourable effects of a forced pace of work. Experience shows that a variety of means can be used in solving these problems. For example, the work can be made more interesting by giving the workers a greater variety of tasks to perform, through multi-skill development and through multi-machine operation.

Many undertakings in the watchmaking, shoe, clothing and other industries are substituting freely paced lines for fixed-pace production lines. As a result the utilisation of working time is improved, labour productivity increases by from 10 to 30 per cent and the unfavourable effects of a forced pace on the individual are eliminated. The use of automated transfer lines has proved especially effective: not only do they enable the unfavourable effects of a forced pace of work to be eliminated, but they also help to reduce the expenditure of labour on carrying out auxiliary activities associated with the finished components.

In view of the limited nature of the possibilities of increasing skills directly on production lines, some undertakings also systematically transfer workers from such lines to other work demanding higher skill. For example, in accordance with a pre-established plan the "Fiftieth Anniversary of the USSR" Volga automobile works trains metal workers from the production lines as repairmen and electricians, machine operators as highly skilled adjusters and operators in the toolmaking and repair shops, and so on. Such additional training is provided on the job at the undertaking's expense.

Work brigades

In accordance with Soviet industrial relations principles, one of the basic features of labour co-operation is the development of collective forms of work organisation in which the workers are grouped into so-called "work brigades". To take a personal interest in the over-all outcome of their work, brigade members must be able to see the results of that work: hence the brigades are as a rule organised in such a way as to carry out the full cycle of operations involved, for example, in the manufacture of certain articles or components or the assembly of large units.

The rules governing the work of a brigade and its individual members must allow for autonomy within this basic production group and provide an opportunity for all members of the brigade to demonstrate their abilities and to satisfy their need for creative development. To meet these requirements the brigades are allowed to arrange for their members to take turns in carrying out the various operations and to give material and moral support to those workers who make the most valuable contribution to the brigade's output, assist their fellow workers and enjoy well deserved authority.

A necessary condition for the successful development of collective work is the creation of a favourable psychological climate within the brigade. This can be helped by the proper selection of the brigade members. As a rule, they are chosen in such a way as to include both experienced workers and young ones and to ensure that an atmosphere of mutual respect and goodwill is established among them. Relations between the members of the brigade are usually not limited to the workplace; they spend their leisure time together, organise group visits to theatres, concerts and film showings and take part in sports meetings and other organised group leisure activities on days off.

The experience of industrial undertakings shows that as a result of the switch to the system of work brigades both labour productivity and the workers' remuneration are increased. This is due to a better use of working time and the favourable conditions created for improving the workers' skills.

Depending on the type and nature of production and the form of labour co-operation adopted, the brigades are either specialised, being made up of workers in one trade (e.g. turners, moulders, fitters), or composite, consisting of workers from various trades. The brigades either work individual shifts, if all their members are on the one shift, or they may operate continuously if they include workers on all shifts.

The widespread adoption of collective forms of work organisation is directly linked with scientific and technological progress. Efficient use of large units and of automated and semi-automated lines depends on the proper co-ordination of the work of all personnel taking part in the production process and the subordination of the work schedule of each individual to the common task, that of ensuring the fullest use of equipment with the least expenditure of labour. Experience has shown that work brigades are the best means of meeting these requirements. Collective forms of work organisation are not used only in industries in which the equipment cannot be operated by one worker (mining, the metal trades and the chemical industry); in recent years dozens of other undertakings in engineering and light industry have switched over to collective forms of work organisation.

Besides the general advantages of collective forms of work organisation mentioned above there are also specific advantages attached to different kinds of work brigades. For example, in engineering undertakings using mass or batch production techniques, specialised brigades of machine operators enable better use to be made of the working time of the highly skilled workers who perform the most complex tasks within the brigade and pass on their experience to the younger workers. The organisation of continuous shift brigades also provides substantial improvements in the use of working time through reduction of the time lost at the start and end of shifts. In the continuous shift brigades the equipment is handed over to the relieving crew without loss of working time. Composite brigades comprising workers of various trades on all shifts are widely used in the extractive industries and in mass line production undertakings in engineering, light industry and food processing, for example. As a rule, such brigades carry out a full module of work in the extraction of minerals or the manufacture of products or components. It is comparatively easy for the workers in composite brigades to master a variety of trades.

The assigning of workers to brigades is worked out beforehand in accordance with the prescribed norms of labour expenditure. Each worker is encouraged to master all the operations assigned to the brigade, and the members of the brigade have an opportunity to change their individual assignments so as to avoid monotony and ensure a better use of working time.

One of the principal current trends in the development of collective work organisation is the transfer of all workers in an undertaking to work in brigades. In recent years this has been done in the Volga automobile works, the Tiraspol clothing factory, the Belebey "Autonormal" Works, the 20th and 23rd State Bearing Works, the Dzhankoy engineering works, the Kherson propeller shaft works and other undertakings.

Multi-machine operation

Scientific and technological progress in industry also requires priority development of other aspects of work organisation suited to a high level of technical equipment and automation of production and to the workers' general and technical education. Such aspects of work organisation include, in particular, multi-machine operation and multi-skilling.

By contributing to a more efficient use of equipment operation time, multi-machine operation provides additional possibilities for increasing labour productivity. It greatly increases the equipment replacement coefficient and improves the efficient usage of the equipment in operation both in individual undertakings and in industry as a whole. Besides the industries in which multi-machine operation has traditionally been used on a wide scale (textiles, food and chemicals), its use has been increasing in recent years in other industries as well, especially engineering. In the most modernised undertakings the proportion of multi-machine operatives is as follows:

Production methods used	*Percentage of multi-machine operatives*
Batch production	30-40
Mass line production	50-70
Partly batch and partly individual production	12-15

In the undertakings concerned the development of multi-machine operation is helped by such necessary preliminary measures as improving the workers' skills, calculating the number of machines that can be operated and serviced, the provision of material and moral incentives and the development of socialist emulation. Experience in those undertakings has shown that the development of multi-machine operation is aided by—

(a) modernisation of machines, which paves the way for automation of the manufacturing cycle and the reduction of the expenditure of manual and machine-handling work time;

(b) improving the construction of equipment with a view to reducing the time spent in auxiliary work, and in particular the adoption of bin feeding of equipment;

(c) improving the layout of equipment to reduce the walking distance involved and to ensure that multi-machine operators have a clear view of all the machines;

(d) the installation of signals to show when a machine needs maintenance;

(e) mechanising such functions as the cleansing of workplaces, the removal of waste materials and the lubrication of equipment;

(f) improving maintenance facilities and programmes; and

(g) introducing group forms of work organisation.

The optimum number of machines that can be attended to by a worker is calculated in two ways. First, the optimal work load is determined for a worker doing active work (machine handling and manual work, active control of the technological process, moving around the work premises). Secondly, the economically sound norms for operating and servicing the machines are determined in the light of the expenditure of human and mechanical labour.

The first group of calculations is based on psychological studies. The number of machines is determined in such a way that the worker has small breaks during the work to allow for additional rest (over and above the established breaks) and to prevent excessive fatigue. On the basis of research findings the proportion of time actually worked in multi-machine operation in the engineering industry has been established as follows:

General purpose machines other than automatic and semi-automatic machines, 0.7-0.8;

Special purpose machines and automatic and semi-automatic machines, including those used on production lines, 0.8.

The main point of the economic calculations is to find out what number of machines corresponds to the minimum total expenditure on production of the product. The calculations take into account those components of the cost price of the product whose value depends on the number of machines being operated, i.e. the sum of the costs connected with the remuneration of production workers (S_{pw}) and with the amortisation and upkeep of equipment (S_e). The relationship between costs and the number of machines in operation is represented in the accompanying figure.

A current trend in industry is to combine the development of multi-machine operation and group work organisation: the number of machines operated by a team is considerably greater than the number of team members. By comparison with individual work organisation, organisation of work in teams leads to a considerable reduction in the amount of equipment standing idle pending maintenance. In addition there are more opportunities for increasing the workers' skills and using all the advantages of group work organisation described above. This type of work organisation has been widely introduced in undertakings in the heavy engineering and automobile sectors.

Relationship between total costs and the number of machines in operation

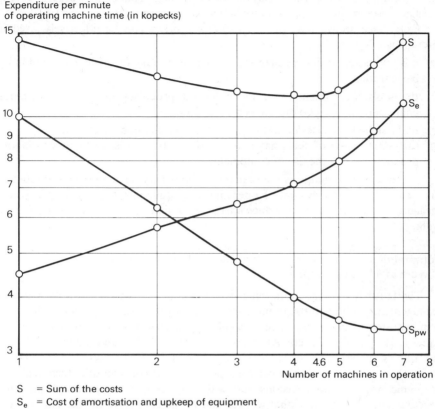

Expenditure per minute
of operating machine time (in kopecks)

S   = Sum of the costs
S_e = Cost of amortisation and upkeep of equipment
S_{pw} = Cost of remuneration of production workers

The present system of remuneration in the USSR provides additional material incentives for multi-machine operators. These incentives are proportionate to output above the norm, and place multi-machine operators in an advantageous position by comparison with other workers.

Multi-skilling

Another development that facilitates automation is multi-skilling. The multi-skilled worker carries out duties connected with his basic trade and also a whole range of jobs linked with other trades, as a result of which fuller use is made of working time and equipment. The work becomes more varied and interesting and the worker's skill is increased. In addition, multi-skilled workers receive in the form of additional wages a considerable proportion of the savings made by the undertaking as a result of the reduction in the labour expenditure on production.

Diversification of skills and functions is practised in both individual and collective work. In many undertakings 20 to 50 per cent of all workers are multi-skilled. Depending on the organisational and technical conditions in the undertaking, the multi-skilled may be found among production workers, among auxiliary workers or among workers in both categories.

Experience shows that the multi-skilled worker can be effectively used in circumstances where—

(a) it is impossible or inexpedient for the worker to take on a full workload in his basic trade;

(b) the tools, instruments and technological processes used share common characteristics and no distances are involved;

(c) multi-skilled activities do not clash with each other over time; and

(d) the combination of skills has had a positive effect on such factors as labour productivity and the use of equipment.

To meet these conditions the sequence of jobs may be altered, new equipment may be installed, the system of operating the equipment may be modified and measures may be taken to reduce distances which multi-skilled workers must walk.

Comprehensive introduction of the scientific organisation
of work in a large enterprise

The feasibility of the comprehensive, simultaneous introduction of scientific management methods throughout a single large enterprise has been convincingly demonstrated by the experience of a pioneering undertaking in Soviet industry, namely the Volga ("Fiftieth Anniversary of the USSR") automobile works. In introducing the scientific organisation of work at the Volga automobile works, a comprehensive approach has been adopted with a firm scientific, technical and economic basis for all decisions and with emphasis on the thorough personal development of each individual worker and of the entire workforce. The process had been preceded by a critical assessment of the existing pattern of work organisation.

This factory is one of the largest in the country's automobile industry. It accounts for over half the Soviet output of passenger cars. The plant is relatively new, having been built between 1967 and 1970; a large town had been constructed near by at the same time to house the workers. The plant is equipped with the most up-to-date machinery. Handling, loading, unloading and stacking operations are fully mechanised and automated.

Youth is a distinctive feature of the factory's workforce; a large proportion of the workers took production jobs after building the factory. Moreover, most of the subsequent recruits have been young people who had completed their secondary education. Because of the workforce's high general educational standard, it is necessary to pay constant attention to job content, so as to ensure that it matches personal preferences and provides prospects of skill development and job satisfaction.

The outcome of the introduction of the scientific organisation of work has been a steady rise in the efficiency of the factory, high production quality, and the development of the workers' potential in the occupational and other fields.

Work brigades

It was decided to organise all the workers in the factory into work brigades. At present, the main plant together with its ancillary factories employs 2,610 of these brigades, comprising 77,400 workers. The work of the brigades in the plant is based on careful technical and economic preparation of all organisation decisions. In particular the work input standards are scientifically determined for every individual and for the plant as a whole. Subject to compliance with the methods of work provided for in the plan, the brigades are responsible for arranging the equipment in their operating areas; determining the optimum sequence of operations within each brigade and the most efficient combination of operations to be performed by each individual, the jobs that can be performed by women and young workers without injury to their health, the optimum pace of work and any changes in pace during the shift, and the skill requirements for brigade members; providing the necessary technical and organisational facilities; and establishing inter-worker links in accordance with the principles of the scientific organisation of work.

Members of a work brigade are generally engaged either in a complete cycle of processing or assembly operations or in a particular stage of production, intermediate inspection being limited. Generally, the brigades are organised in the former way on short automated production lines, and in the latter way on the main assembly lines and long automated production lines.

In auxiliary production wide use is made not only of the cycle method but also of specialised brigades consisting, for example, of lathe or milling-machine operators.

The sense of responsibility felt by the individual worker towards his group and the group's concern over the work of each individual are strengthened by the principle of having workers in both shifts in one group, i.e. through the organisation of "cross-over brigades".

The advantage of work brigades (or "the collective organisation of work" as it is called) introduced at the Volga automobile works is that it gives the workers a real interest in all or the greater part of the work done by their brigade. This attitude is also fostered by the system of payment, which includes a skill bonus, assessed on the basis of the quality of the work actually peformed and the number of operations mastered by the worker. Achievement of a higher standard of skill not only makes it possible to enhance job content, which in itself is extremely important in assembly-line mass production, but also facilitates the spread of multi-machine operation. Not only does the work brigade system in the factory promote collective responsibility for the implementation of the production plan, but it actively affects relations within the group, since the allocation of the bonuses for the contribution made by each member of a brigade to the common result, and the selection of the best workers for material and moral encouragement, are both the outcome of collective decisions.

Calculation of the results of the brigade's work and payment on the basis of the operations completed ensures collective responsibility for output and promotes solidarity within the brigades, creating a painstaking, helpful attitude. This is particularly important whenever newcomers join a brigade. Not only do they feel their responsibility towards the group to do their jobs rapidly and well, but they find that they can always rely on help from the more experienced and skilled members of the group.

Incentives

Great importance is attached in this plant to socialist emulation as an invaluable factor in raising productive efficiency and educating the workers in an active, creative approach to their jobs. The distinctive feature of socialist emulation in the Volga automobile works is that it takes place in conditions of steadily flowing production, which has been built up to its optimum rate, and is extremely well balanced as between one department and another. The factory's output norms all have a technical basis and optimum work norms are assigned to each work brigade on the basis of the factory's output norms. Accordingly, emulation within the factory mainly involves implementing the plan with the least waste of materials and labour, while maintaining the high quality standards.

It is essential to achieve the right combination of moral and material incentives if there is to be extensive participation by the workers in socialist emulation. The traditional systems of moral incentives comprised a whole array of methods which emphasised such things as certificates, diplomas and pennants. Research has shown, however, that they are less satisfactory in meeting the workers' need for moral approval by the staff as a whole than systems based on the award of honorary titles for a period of a year (for example: "Winner of emulation competition", "Leading worker") or several years ("Veteran brigade member", "Honoured worker"). Each honorary title awarded to a worker is a symbol of moral encouragement and a form of publicity given to social approval. Similarly, brigades winning socialist emulation competitions are awarded "certificates of quality" that are valid for a period ranging from a month to a year. Every brigade receives a bonus of up to 20 per cent of the basic wage for as long as it holds such a certificate. It is now customary for 97 per cent of all the brigades in the factory to compete for the certificate.

Brigade committees and production meetings

In order to enlarge the range of questions decided by the work brigades and involve a greater number of workers, the management, jointly with the plant trade union committee, has drawn up and approved a set of rules for production brigade committees. At present there are some 1,200 brigade committees in the plant, with a membership of over 7,000. These committees discuss the progress of socialist emulation, moral and material rewards for the winners of emulation contests, production quality and attitudes, labour discipline and the general conduct of brigade members, and the selection of candidates for upgrading.

In order to eliminate lack of interest in the work and strengthen social supervision over the execution of the factory's commitments, the draft commitments for the coming year are explained at public meetings. For each commitment, an investigation is made to see how far it is justified in practical terms, and to what extent it reflects the true production capacity of the individual worker or the workforce.

Each worker upholds his proposed individual target before his brigade committee, the brigade committee before the workshop committee, the workshop committee before the production committee, and the production committee before the central factory committee. The committees are composed of representatives of the social organisations, heads of subdivisions, prominent specialists and leading workers. The specialists attending meetings of brigade committees to investigate production problems usually report that it is easier to discuss things with the factory manager than with the workers.

An important feature of the brigade committees is that they function throughout the year, and are under an obligation to check on the fulfilment of commitments and to give any necessary assistance to participants in emulation contests. In addition to production targets (on such matters as reduction in all forms of waste, improvement in product quality, raising of workers' skill standards and savings in raw materials) it is usual for production brigades taking part in such contests to assume a wide range of obligations under the welfare plan, such as the raising of the workers' general educational and cultural standards, sponsorship of trainees, and assistance in the building and improvement of the city and factory.

The efforts of the brigade committees lead to higher technical standards and better industrial attitudes, more active participation by the workers in industrial and social life, and the growth of a feeling of interdependence and responsibility. In the view of the workers themselves, most of the problems arising within their brigades are now dealt with more objectively.

Economic and social education

During the ninth (1971-75) five-year plan, an economic education scheme covered 80 per cent of the workers actually employed in production. To organise and operate the scheme in the factory, an economic education committee has been set up, comprising prominent specialists, representatives of social organisations and outstanding workers.

The factory has prepared a three-volume textbook on the economics of the Volga automobile works. In addition, a monthly bulletin publishes the plant's technical and economic performance statistics for the benefit of those concerned with the current results of the efforts of all the people working in the plant. Special facilities, including a wide range of visual aids, are provided for classes and seminars under this scheme.

Education of the workers in creative activity, and the development of socio-political consciousness within the plant workforce, constitute major features of general economic education. Such education is regarded as an essential part of upgrading training and is taken into account for the grant of a title or certificate and for promotion to the ranks of engineering, technical or non-manual staff.

The success of the measures taken to improve the factory's workforce has been facilitated by a constant improvement in the social information provided through a series of monthly social information bulletins dealing with clearly defined social problems. The themes of the bulletins correspond to the sections of the social development plan and are repeated every year, thereby providing an opportunity to follow the dynamics of the social process and to analyse the nature of the changes taking place in the plant.

Any worker can obtain a detailed explanation on any subject connected with working and living conditions from the factory and production managers at meetings organised by 14 social and political clubs that have been set up within the factory in order to ensure that workers derive full benefit from their time off and achieve maximum cultural development. The clubrooms can cater for roughly 350 people. In addition to the traditional lectures, meetings are organised with literary and scientific figures and experienced workers, talks are given on artistic, literary and technical publications, popular science films are shown, and functions are held in honour of workers with long records of service. The chairman of the committee of the club in the body assembly department is a paint worker, L. Yuzhno, while in the mechanical assembly department he is a radio reporter, M. Shabunin.

Improvement of the working and social environment

To improve working conditions in the plant, special attention is devoted to achieving optimum psycho-physiological standards, on the basis of research carried out by the factory physiology and psychology laboratory into such matters as the effects of working conditions on workers' physique and on patterns of fatigue during the working day. For example, on the laboratory's recommendation, changes are made in the speed of the main assembly line during the working day. Ten-minute rest breaks are also given after every two hours worked on the line. At present, the laboratory is planning the introduction of background music in the workshops, and individual receivers with headphones are being provided in areas where the noise level is high.

Since the factory started operations, every effort has been made by the conditions of work section to design and implement measures to safeguard the workers' health and reduce fatigue. Apart from general health measures, the section has concentrated on gradually eliminating adverse factors in the workshops and improving the working environment. Thus, bars where the workers are served oxygenated albuminous vitaminised beverages are being opened in growing numbers throughout the factory. As examples of general health measures, it may be mentioned that gymnastics are performed at the place of work during the first regulation break for a snack and hot beverage, and under the sports and health scheme, which operates both inside and outside the factory, workers are issued with vouchers for stays in preventive care clinics, rest homes, sanatoria, holiday homes and one-day rest centres. The bulk of the cost of these vouchers is met out of funds made available by the factory trade union committee.

In conjunction with a number of scientific research institutes, the conditions of work section is constantly studying and assessing working conditions of individual work stations, work areas and workshops, and draws up current and long-term plans for the improvement of the working environment. At present, this programme covers 23,000 work stations, involving 45,600 workers. Measures to improve working conditions are thus continuous and specific. About 1.5 million roubles are allocated every year to finance a major effort to reduce noise and vibration levels, to improve the working environment, and to forecast or eliminate detrimental environmental factors due to the introduction of new materials and technical processes.

Vocational selection and training

For the selection of workers for particularly monotonous and demanding jobs, the factory has developed medico-biological and psychological criteria of suitability for the main occupations. The factory has a vocational selection department, where after a medical examination young people are interviewed by specialists—physiologists, psychologists and sociologists—who, on the basis of tests, advise them in their choice of the occupation best suited to their individual characteristics.

Another feature is the upgrading scheme, involving career planning and continuous training for assembly-line workers to fit them for highly skilled jobs (as toolmakers, adjusters, maintenance men) on the basis of their personal preferences, practical aptitudes, moral qualities and participation in public affairs.

Introduction of the scientific organisation of work on an industry-wide basis*

The manufacture of textiles is one of the biggest industries in the USSR, in terms both of the size of workforce employed and of the number of undertakings. Organisational and technical patterns and trends in this industry have a specific character that is all their own. For decades the textiles industry continued to use traditional techniques and technology even though output and the speed of production were constantly rising. It is only recently that major qualitative changes have occurred as a result of an energetic policy of introducing new and indeed revolutionary equipment, and partially or fully automated production lines. Textile undertakings are being equipped with pneumatic spinning machines; spinning-and-twisting machines which combine the processes of spinning, winding, throwing and twisting; pneumatic looms; pneumatic rapier weaving machines; and mechanised and automated production lines in preparatory spinning shops, in finishing, and so on. In addition, various novel types of textile products are now being produced on an industrial scale.

Side by side with radical changes in the technical base of the textiles industry, there have been important changes in the composition of its workforce. In the five years from 1970 to 1975 the number of specialists[1] who had obtained diplomas of higher or specialised secondary education increased by 32 per cent, and in the ten years from 1965 to 1975 their numbers doubled. Recent years have been marked by a rapid rise in the workers' levels of general education and vocational training.

The improvement in material living conditions and in the workers' general education and culture are accompanied by a general rise in requirements as regards working conditions and efficient organisation of production. This is a

---

* The authors of this case study are A. Dovba, N. Kochkina and V. Kochetkov, all of the Labour Research Institute.

particularly important factor in shaping the organisation of work, especially in the textile industry, because the textile industry has to compete for labour with new, non-traditional industries such as electronics, radio and television, precision mechanics and optics. The industries which have sprung up or have been rapidly developed on the basis of the latest achievements of science and technology are seen by young workers with secondary education as providing opportunities for using their knowledge, as affording good prospects for personal development and as offering jobs with higher prestige. Hence in conditions of full employment the recruitment of young people into the textile industry can be improved only if radical changes are made in working conditions and in the organisation of work so as to provide interesting and creative jobs.

All this has led to radical changes in the organisational and technical conditions of production. The following are some of the main changes:

(1) The reduction of the length of production cycles and the number of processing stages has been accompanied by an increasing continuity of processes.

(2) There has been an increase in the work pace, in the thoroughness with which the work is done, and in the size of packages.

(3) The number of disturbances of the technological process (breaks in yarn or fabric, breakdowns of machinery) has been reduced thanks to the use of improved mechanical methods of increasing manufacturing reliability and precision.

(4) There has been a transfer of auxiliary operations from man to machine and of a substantial proportion of the operations involved in regulating the flow of the technological process to automatic equipment and instruments through the installation of fully automated shops, sections, lines and a substantial stock of machines and equipment with pre-set controls.

(5) Maximum comfort, safety, health and efficiency in the operation and control of the equipment are being ensured by observing the requirements of the scientific organisation of work in the design and planning of production premises.

Work organisation models and improvements in equipment of work stations

The application to the textile industry of the most important work organisation measures adopted for the economy as a whole is mainly carried out by the Scientific Work Organisation Centre for Light Industry in the Central Scientific Research Institute of Information and Technical and Economic Research of the USSR Ministry of Light Industry. The Scientific Work Organisation Centre and the subordinate scientific research institutes for the cotton, wool, silk, linen, haberdashery and knitted-goods industries and others have devised and applied work organisation models for more than 200 occupations in which large numbers of workers are employed. These schemes cover efficient methods of planning work stations and equipping them with various aids and fittings, lifting and transporting equipment, tools and minor items of machinery; the division of labour, joint work assignments and efficient methods of work; the servicing of work stations and communications; occupational safety and health, work and rest schedules, and the provision of protective clothing and footwear.

Models for the organisation of work and work stations have been drawn up for all basic trades in textile production such as weavers, spinners, operators working on mechanised and automated lines, and so on. The use of these models has contributed considerably to the improvement of working conditions and labour productivity.

For example, the model for the organisation of the work station of a weaver in the silk industry working on P-125A pneumatic looms covers the best possible division of labour in the workshop and efficient methods of work. The introduction of such machines in place of shuttle looms and the mastering of the new working methods suggested by the model resulted in a fivefold or sixfold increase in the weavers' labour productivity (the number of looms minded per worker rose from 12 to between 52 and 75).

The model for the organisation of the work station of a weaver in the wool industry working on carpet weaving machines suggested a variety of general measures to make the work much easier and to improve labour productivity considerably. The work station was equipped with a revolving chair which could be raised or lowered and an adjustable foot-board on the machine. These devices enable the weaver to keep a watchful eye on the work of the machine while remaining seated and ensure a comfortable working position while breaks in the yarn warp are mended from the front of the loom. The weavers' efficiency is considerably increased not only by efficient technical equipment of the work station but also by other measures suggested in the scheme for reducing fatigue—additional ten-minute regulation rest breaks two hours before the end of the shift, a hot meal on the night shift, foot baths and self-massage, background music, and the provision of comfortable, hygienic and attractive work clothing and shoes. Studies carried out in one undertaking where these models were introduced—a group of carpet-weaving factories that are established in Moscow—show that where previously weavers spent 15 per cent more time at the end of the shift than at the beginning on performing a specific task selected by the physiologists for assessing level of fatigue, the difference was reduced to only 1 per cent after the measures suggested by the model had been implemented; there was also an improvement in the indicators of strength and endurance of the arm and back muscles. The time taken by weavers to perform basic operations was reduced on average by almost 20 per cent; labour productivity increased 15 per cent (after the model was introduced the hourly output of a weaver rose from 5.9 to 7.1 square metres).

Wide use has been made of work organisation charts. These are condensed versions of the work organisation model, and list the recommended sequence of the workers' activities, the methods of work, the work norms, the organisation of the work station and its servicing, the conditions of work and the remuneration system. Observance of the norms laid down in these charts is compulsory, and any deviation is regarded as an infringement of discipline.

Many items of equipment for work stations in the textile industry are developed and produced centrally. For example, the following items are mass-produced: technological packages with spring-actuated bottoms which facilitate the work of the drawer and improve the quality of half-finished products in linen production; AOSP-1 automatic fluff collectors for the work stations of winders in wool production, and various other pieces of mechanised equipment for continuous servicing of work stations and for removing fluff and dust from the machinery, the walls and ceilings of production premises and the ventilation and light fittings.

Work stations for the general run of workers have also undergone technical adjustment to improve working posture and make the work easier. Winding machines are equipped with comfortable worker-controlled stools which move along the front of the spindles. These have been installed, for instance, for winders in the Kherson group of cotton mills and in many other cotton undertakings. In the "Red Profintern" spinning and weaving factory, winders move from one machine to another on mechanised stools and the women may at will alternate between sitting and standing. Mobile stools are used by weavers and workers in jobs which traditionally call for prolonged and constant movement. The Darnitsa group of silk undertakings uses special equipment to move weavers operating the P-125A pneumatic machines. This equipment consists of a fenced platform with seats; the platform is on wheels with rubber tyres which are set in motion by an electric motor under continuous supply from a trolley contact mains. The introduction of this equipment has made the work substantially easier and improved labour productivity thanks to a considerable reduction in the idle time of machines. The results of a special survey conducted with the platform moving at an average speed of between 1.8 and 3 metres per second (as compared with 0.4-0.6 metres per second without a platform) showed that the reduction in the idle time of machines amounted to 28 and 36 per cent respectively. Constant efforts to improve workplaces and ease the work are being made in undertakings such as the Podmoskovie group of undertakings which produce woollen children's fabrics, the Krengolm textile mill at Narva, the Mozdok curtain factory, the Ulan-Ude group of fine cloths mills, the I. N. Akimov fine cloths mill at Kupava, the Rabochy weaving and spinning mill in Leningrad, the Andizhan cotton mill and many others.

In the majority of textile undertakings using multi-machine operation a signalling and communications system is used to call the assistant foreman, the equipment adjuster or auxiliary workers and to ask for the necessary half-finished products and materials. This cuts down the work of the servicing staff and ensures reliability in the supply of the work station with everything that is needed. Work stations are linked to a control centre. For example, in the "Red Rose" Rosa Luxemburg group of woollen mills in Moscow, automated installations of the "Signal" type control the work of the looms, record their idle times and output, and provide communications between the foremen and assistant foremen and the work stations. The instruments transmit signals and information to a central control desk from which they are fed into an electronic computer for processing.

Many types of modern textile equipment cannot be operated efficiently by a single worker; production losses occur if a machine is idle until a worker can attend to it, and such losses increase in proportion to the speed of processing. Team work is therefore of growing importance as a result of the introduction of high efficiency techniques, and is widely used in the textile industry. As in other industries, teams may be composed of workers who are either all in the one trade or are multi-skilled. As a rule, a team is headed by an assistant foreman whose duties include adjusting and making minor repairs to the technical equipment.

The foregoing account must not be taken to mean that all the problems involved in improving the organisation of the work stations of textile workers have been fully solved. In the current five-year period 22 per cent of work stations were organised in accordance with work organisation models and 70 per cent were equipped with the necessary aids and fittings. By 1980, however, it is planned that 40 per cent of work stations will be organised in accordance with work organisation models and 85 per cent provided with modern aids and fittings meeting all the requirements of the scientific organisation of work.

Job improvement through work reorganisation

One particularly important problem now confronting the textile industry in the USSR is the need to make work more interesting in order to attract labour. It can be asserted with certainty that in the very near future the industry will be fully able to guarantee favourable working conditions thanks to technical and organisational measures and the all-round mechanisation of arduous and time-consuming jobs. At the same time, priority will be given to the question of job satisfaction. In the long run, especially in view of the increasing difficulties of attracting staff, job satisfaction will become a major factor in the future development of any branch of production.

If one considers the general trends in the development of the technological base of the textile industry in the USSR the prospects for the future look good. Even now the following trends are clearly apparent: jobs are being made more interesting; the difference between physical and mental work is narrowing; and individual work is increasingly giving way to team work.

Quantitative assessment of the degree of interest of a job is of considerable assistance in the social and economic analysis of characteristic features of modern textile production. Research carried out in the textile industry of the USSR has brought to light changes in jobs as a result of technological developments, and has enabled those changes to be evaluated in quantitative terms. In carrying out this research original methods were used. First, the work of each worker in a factory (whether a key or auxiliary worker, a team leader, a foreman, a member of the engineering staff or a non-manual worker) was studied according to a common plan. Secondly, the content of all workers' jobs were viewed as the aggregate of the tasks they performed. Thirdly, the degree of interest of the work was evaluated in terms of the complexity of the tasks performed by the worker concerned, the amount, complexity and novelty of the information used, the type of decisions involved, and a number of other factors. The amount of information was measured by the volume of communications (in nominal units); its complexity according to the variety and number of the signs or indications and its novelty according to the proportion of non-recurring communications. Decisions were classified into three kinds—stereotyped (with a rigid algorithm), diagnostic (with an adjustable algorithm) and heuristic (non-algorithmised).

Tables 1 and 2 provide information illustrating how jobs have been made more interesting through technical re-equipment (with an identical workload over time). The proportion of diagnostic decisions taken by foremen in spinning and weaving shops is increasing and the information used by them is becoming substantially more complex. However, the most significant improvements in the degree of interest of job content are to be found among manual workers: the proportion of diagnostic decisions taken by spinners increases from 2 per cent to 15 per cent, and by weavers from 6 per cent (automatic shuttles) to 16 per cent, with a corresponding drop in the proportion of stereotyped decisions calling for very little mental effort.

An analysis of the information used on the job reveals that the degree of interest of the job is improving at a faster rate for manual workers (weavers and spinners) than for assistant foremen, and particularly for full foremen. While for assistant foremen the level of novelty of information rises from 35 per cent to 60 per cent in spinning and from 50 per cent to 80 per cent in weaving, and in the case of foremen from 60-65 per cent to 80-90 per cent, for the manual workers operating weaving equipment the proportion of new data nearly trebles. The trend towards a reduction in the volume and an increase in the complexity of the data used on the introduction of more advanced techniques is common to all categories of workers but most marked in the case of manual workers. These tables confirm that the gap between the work of supervisors and manual workers is narrowing as the latter are being given increasingly creative tasks to perform.

With the increased complexity and higher productivity of the technology, highly skilled team leaders, assistant foremen and senior workers are drawing closer to the process of supervision and control, and their functions as leaders of small groups of workers are emerging more clearly. At the same time the work of manual workers tending the machines is being rendered more complex and being enriched with more varied and new information. A significant part of their work now consists in controlling the equipment and the technological process.

Particularly important changes have taken place in the work of manual workers as a result of automation. In the cotton industry the use of automated combined carding-and-drawing units instead of separate carding and drawing machines has made jobs more interesting. For example, the operator of one of the new units uses twice the variety of information that the carders and drawers used on the old equipment. The proportion of new and non-recurring items of information conveyed to the operator is more than 20 per cent, as against 6 per cent in the case of carders on traditional machines. The diversity of information increases three-and-a-half times for assistant foremen in automated units and two-and-a-half times for foremen in these shops.

A uniform approach to the assessment of all work processes in terms of the complexity and structure of the production tasks performed allows comparisons

Table 1. Characteristics of job content in spinning shops with different kinds of technical equipment

Occupation	Type of equipment	Structure of job content (as percentage of time spent)—				Characteristics of information used		
		by type of task		by type of decision		Volume (thousands nominal units)		Variety (total number of indications)
		Control	Operative	Stereo-typed	Diagnostic	Total	Of which: non-recurring communica-tions	
Foreman	Ring	100	0	10	90	12.5	8.2	910
	Pneumatic	100	0	5	95	10.1	9.1	1 320
Assistant foreman	Ring	30	70	40	60	5.2	1.85	180
	Pneumatic	35	65	30	70	3.8	2.3	270
Spinner	Ring	5	95	98	2	3.0	0.35	51
	Pneumatic	9	91	85	15	1.8	0.62	103

Table 2. Characteristics of job content in weaving shops with different kinds of technical equipment

Occupation	Type of equipment	Structure of job content (as percentage of time spent)—				Characteristics of information used		
		by type of task		by type of decision		Volume (thousands of nominal units)		Variety (total number of indications)
		Control	Oper-ative	Stereo-typed	Diag-nostic	Total	Of which: non-recurring communica-tions	
Foreman	Mechanical shuttle	100	0	22	78	18.0	11.0	670
	Automatic shuttle	100	0	11	89	12.2	9.1	960
	Automatic pneumatic rapier	100	0	5	95	11.0	8.8	1 100
Assistant foreman	Mechanical shuttle	8	92	50	50	4.6	2.3	230
	Automatic shuttle	18	82	39	61	3.6	2.3	380
	Automatic pneumatic rapier	21	79	26	74	3.1	2.55	490
Weaver	Mechanical shuttle	0	100	100	0	3.4	0.34	43
	Automatic shuttle	5	95	94	6	2.8	0.28	76
	Automatic pneumatic rapier	8	92	84	16	1.8	0.55	118

to be made among individual workplaces, and also allows the entire work process in a section or shop to be studied at greater length and in greater depth. To assess the level and structure of the total expenditure of labour it is necessary for the work of all workers to be measured in terms of a common unit; under this system the labour expenditure of individual workers is given a proportionate weighting in the over-all sum of labour expenditure.

Table 3. Structure of production tasks performed by groups in spinning and weaving shops
(Percentage distribution of working time)

Type of workshop	Control tasks			
	Controlling means of production		Controlling work performance	Total
	Technological process	Equipment		
Spinning shop equipped with—				
ring machines	2.5	1.9	2.4	6.8
pneumatic machines	3.3	3.2	3.3	9.8
Weaving shop equipped with—				
mechanical looms	1.0	1.0	2.8	4.8
automatic looms	2.2	2.3	2.6	7.1
pneumatic looms	4.0	2.9	2.5	9.4

The equipment of spinning shops with new technology has altered the nature of the work done (see table 3).

With the introduction of new spinning equipment the correlation between the proportions of control and operative tasks has changed (6.8 and 93.2 per cent respectively in ring spinning and 9.8 and 90.2 per cent in pneumatic spinning). The increase in the proportion of control tasks is accompanied by qualitative improvements, particularly in the work of manual workers. All tasks performed by foremen and heads of shops on new and old equipment are control tasks; for manual workers operating more complex and more productive equipment the proportion of control tasks increases. Thus, for spinners the proportion of control tasks amounts to 6.2 per cent of working time when operating ring spinners and 7.9 per cent when working on pneumatic machines; for doffers control tasks make up 2.2 and 2.6 per cent of the time, respectively. An important qualitative change in the nature of work done in spinning shops is the considerable increase in the proportion of machine-minding and preventive functions. With the switch-over to pneumatic spinning machines the proportion of these functions increased from 34.4 to 36.8 per cent while the proportion of tasks connected with emergencies dropped from 25.9 to 21.1 per cent respectively. This obviously has a positive effect in that more of the work proceeds according to plan.

The same trends are revealed in the structure of production tasks in weaving shops with different levels of technology. The proportion of control tasks increases from 4.8 per cent for mechanical equipment to 9.4 per cent for pneumatic machines. The rise occurs in tasks connected with controlling the technological process (from 1 to 4 per cent) and equipment (from 1 to 2.9 per cent). On the other hand there is some reduction in the time spent on dealing with personnel problems (work performance). Important changes take place in the structure of operative tasks. As a result of improvements in the equipment there is a steady and sharp fall in the proportion of tasks connected with feeding the

Operative tasks

Servicing the technological process					Servicing equipment and work stations		Total
Minding or preventive work				Dealing with emergencies	Minding or preventive work	Dealing with emergencies	
Feeding	Doffing	Transporting	Checking				
5.7	16.2	8.2	4.3	25.9	28.4	4.5	93.2
7.7	6.3	11.0	11.8	21.1	28.1	4.2	90.2
20.5	3.6	3.8	15.3	22.0	18.0	12.0	95.2
14.7	5.1	4.1	16.4	22.3	19.5	10.8	92.9
6.8	5.6	4.2	17.8	22.4	27.0	6.8	90.6

machines with half-finished products: automatic loading of the shuttle with spools enables the proportion of time spent on this type of work to be reduced from 20.5 to 14.7 per cent and the introduction of a fixed weft package has enabled it to be reduced to 6.8 per cent. At the same time the proportion of checking operations rises from 15.3 to 16.4 and 17.8 per cent, respectively.

Such, then, are the changes in the nature of the work done by the manufacturing personnel. It can be inferred that with the introduction of new and more advanced techniques the work is becoming more complex technically and that its distribution among the workers is changing. Increased complexity is a feature of the work of manual workers, as well as of supervisors and engineering staff. Calculations show that in weaving, preparatory spinning and spinning shops as well as in a number of other textile production sections, when new techniques have been introduced and have been sufficiently mastered the nature of the work done by assistant foremen, whose functions include adjusting the equipment, is substantially changed. For this category of worker the proportion of control tasks increases as a result of the introduction of more complex equipment. Thus, for assistant foremen the time spent on control tasks amounts to 5.2 per cent on a set of mechanical looms, 9 per cent on automatic looms and 11.5 per cent on pneumatic looms.

A particularly important fact to be noted is the increasingly substantial proportion of control tasks being performed by machine operators as a result of the introduction of new techniques. Whereas the control activities of a carder amount to 2.3 per cent and of a drawer to 2 per cent, in the case of an operator of a carding-and-drawing unit they amount to 10 per cent.

All these moves to make work more interesting and reduce the gap between physical and mental labour make for social equality among the various categories of personnel, in conformity with socialist principles.

Study of job content in a number of major textile undertakings in the USSR with the aid of a quantitative assessment of the degree of interest of the work has made it possible to establish a number of rules which can be used in designing efficient forms of work organisation for the present day. These rules take account of the quantitative relationship between the organisational and technical characteristics of production and the complexity of the tasks of the control and supervisory staff; of the implications of job content from the point of view of control and the information system; and of organisational principles governing the formation of efficient small work groups.

Beside improving rate-fixing for individual jobs, efforts are being made to develop methods of rate-fixing for groups. In the textile industry an over-all study of the content of jobs in being made, their degree of interest being assessed on the basis of a study of the complexity of the tasks performed, while psychological and physiological analysis reveals what effects varying degrees of job enrichment have on the individual. This study raises the problem of collecting data on which the quantitative criteria can be based.

The task for the future will be to master methods of controlling and directing the on-going development of the process of making work more interesting in the undertaking and narrowing the gap between physical and mental labour.

CONCLUSIONS

Analysis of new forms of work organisation in the USSR makes it possible to single out dominant trends which result from the long-term development objectives of socialist society. These trends are as follows:

(a) development of group forms of work organisation, providing a suitable combination of the interest of the productive group with the availability of broad possibilities in respect of the all-round development of individual members of the group;

(b) a steady rise in the educational level of the workers, together with an improvement in their qualifications, professional competence and work habits (these improvements increase their ability to deal with the particular problems facing them at present as well as to handle new, more complex, future assignments that will result from scientific and technical progress);

(c) an improvement in conditions of work, and increasing emphasis on its creative nature;

(d) development of a comprehensive approach to the scientific organisation of work in all areas, with a growing concern for the social aspects; and

(e) an integrated approach to the problems of technical improvement, technology, work organisation, production and management.

Note

¹ Under article 45 of the Constitution of the USSR ". . . the right to education . . . is ensured by . . . the institution of universal, compulsory secondary education and broad development of vocational, specialised secondary, and higher education, in which instruction is oriented toward practical activity and production . . .". In practice "specialists" would appear to include managerial and supervisory staff and technicians of all kinds (see "Specialised education in the USSR", in *International Labour Review,* Aug. 1967, pp. 208-209, and also G. Bogatov: "The development of vocational training in the USSR in response to scientific and technical progress", ibid., Dec. 1975, on pp. 468-469).

ECONOMIC COSTS AND BENEFITS

Sign used in the tables: . . . = not available

ECONOMIC COSTS AND BENEFITS OF NEW FORMS OF WORK ORGANISATION

Anthony G. Hopwood*

Recent decades have witnessed a growing concern with the consequences of the routine, repetitive and bureaucratically organised work which characterises so much of employment in a modern industrial society. With changing social and political values and an increasing awareness of the range of possibilities available, it is now realised that a great deal of modern work, whether in the factory or the office, offers little scope for exercising individual initiative and responsibility. People working on these jobs often see their tasks as boring and meaningless; and the effects of this view are now seen as extending far beyond the confines of the individual mind or even of the undertaking which provides employment. The nature of work can and does have wide-ranging implications for the effectiveness of the individual, the enterprise as a whole and the quality of life in society at large.

For a long time it had been assumed that the human and social consequences of work were an inevitable, even if unfortunate, result of modern production methods and the size and complexity of contemporary organisations. According to this view, little could be done to make work more satisfying. However, it is now becoming clear that it is possible to redesign the organisation of work so as to provide greater personal fulfilment without necessarily having to loose the advantages of modern technology.

The realisation that the organisation of work and its consequences are shaped by social as well as technological factors has led to an awareness of the various possible ways of organising work. From the 1950s, and particularly during the 1960s and 1970s, an increasing number of people both in Europe and in the United States started to experiment with different approaches to work organisation (Klein, 1976; Work in America, 1972), ranging from relatively modest rearrangements of the elements of individual jobs to a fundamental restructuring of those patterns of influence and control in organisations that help to determine the selection and use of technology. However diverse they may be, these various approaches all offer some possibility of relating the advances of

---

* Oxford Centre for Management Studies.

modern technology with the achievement of human needs and aspirations. Taken together, they are now starting to play a significant role in shaping our conceptions of the possibilities for the organisation, management and performance of an undertaking.

An emerging interest in evaluation

As was inevitable, many of the early experiments were concerned primarily with practical feasibility. At that stage the most vital point to establish was that different approaches to the social organisation of work could be designed and followed. General claims were made about the over-all effectiveness of such approaches, but their actual existence was important in its own right.

Subsequently a growing body of experience made a more detailed appreciation of the operation and effect of the different forms of work organisation more important. Beyond some point—one that is generally agreed to have been reached, if not passed—further learning and progress become increasingly dependent on understanding the factors that promote or hinder the achievement of the potential offered by the new approaches. The real magnitude and scope of that potential also needs to be delineated; and with an increasing range of possible approaches it becomes important to consider in a reasoned manner their relative strengths and weaknesses and the circumstances in which they are most effective.

Such concerns helped to promote an interest in evaluating the social effectiveness of the new forms of work organisation. Many of the early evaluative attempts were crude and simplistic, but more recently a great deal of effort has been devoted to monitoring the social nature of the change process itself and its human consequences in a more systematic manner. Although numerous problems undoubtedly remain, significant progress has been made. Undertakings now have at their disposal useful and convenient instruments for appraising the effect of different forms of work organisation on individual attitudes and forms of social behaviour (Biderman and Drury, 1976; Portigal, 1974; Portigal, 1976; Seashore, 1976); and an increasing number of undertakings are doing just this.

In contrast, however, the assessment of the economic costs and benefits of programmes designed to improve the quality of working life has been relatively neglected. There has been a tendency for both social innovators and persons professionally concerned with economic measurement to see financial performance and the fulfilment of human needs as two separate areas of concern. Instead of choosing to emphasise the interplay of social, technical and economic forces which itself constitutes an undertaking, these different groups of people have often chosen, albeit implicitly, to emphasise the divergent value bases which might underlie the differing views of an undertaking's effectiveness. Professionals in economic measurement have accordingly emphasised the dominance of existing financial criteria, and in consequence they have often viewed social innovations in an unduly narrow perspective. Conversely, and with few exceptions (Likert, 1967), social innovators have tended to interpret expressions of concern over economic consequences as improper attempts to reinforce past perspectives, options and influences rather than facilitate the process of change.

Accordingly it is not difficult to appreciate why, until recently, there has been little demand for—let alone supply of—appropriate methodologies for economic assessment. What concern there has been with the economic consequences of different forms of work organisation has reflected a desire to legitimise rather than to either assess or learn (Klein, 1976, p. 47).

For these reasons the potential magnitude of the economic consequences of programmes designed to improve the quality of working life is only just being realised. So far both their costs and benefits have invariably been lost within the mass of detailed calculations which give rise to the aggregate assessment of financial outcomes.

However, real and genuine interest is now shown in evaluating the economic consequences of different forms of work organisation. That interest stems from a number of factors. First, there is a growing realisation that the economic aspects of change, or of not changing for that matter, are important. To cite only one example, it is now realised that the replacement of the 100,000 workers leaving the Bell telephone system every year costs over $100 million (Gustafson, 1974). When seen in such terms, it is not only right that programmes directed towards improving the social fabric of the undertaking should be considered alongside programmes concerned with technological, market and financial change; they also need to be analysed in a comparable manner, because they also represent vital ways in which the profitability of the undertaking can be improved. Secondly, it is realised that if changes in work organisation are not analysed in a comparable manner, there is a danger that they may be seen as purely resource-consuming activities rather than potential resource-generating activities; and in those circumstances technological and marketing changes are likely to be given preference over equally profitable programmes concerned with improving the quality of working life. At no time is this more likely to happen than when resources are severely limited, as at present. When there are strong pressures to economise, potentially successful social initiatives can easily be either rejected or abandoned on the ground that they will not pay for themselves.

One such instance has been documented by Weir (1976, pp. 27-29). Despite known improvements in throughput, the amount of work in progress, quality, absenteeism and labour turnover, and greater flexibility of the production process, an autonomous working group experiment in a clothing manufacturing company was abandoned in mid-course. As the general economic situation worsened, a highly visible and immediate increase in unit costs was emphasised at the expense of the other improvements, even though the increase might have reflected the peculiarities of the products being processed at the time and the idiosyncracies as well as partialities of the cost accounting system. In the absence of any attempt to evaluate systematically the over-all economic consequences of the experiment, the influential though partial returns produced by the existing accounting system had a decisive effect on policy.

The need for more general awareness of the economic implications of social change is of fundamental importance. Current programmes for work reorganisation have been based on a concern for moving beyond the damaging fragmentation of perception and understanding which had become so characteristic of our intellectual tradition. Possibilities of overcoming the constraints inherent in modern production technology were created by explicitly considering the relationship between the technological and social structures of enterprises. Further progress might be encouraged by recognising that the domains of economic and social action can never be satisfactorily separated. Our economic structures, perspectives and methodologies have always reflected emerging social values and possibilities. Instead of imposing stronger economic constraints on social progress, an awareness of the interplay between social and economic advances within the undertaking can generate further suggestions for future progress (Likert, 1967; Vanek, 1970, 1971). Today's difficult economic conditions only serve to increase the need for and potential of such a wider approach.

Costs and benefits classified

It is useful to classify the economic costs and benefits of work reorganisation programmes into three broad categories: the operational, the systemic and the societal.

Operational

The concept of operational consequences covers the effect that the organisation of work has on the regular operating flows of an enterprise. The differing requirements for personnel and materials, the financial implications of these, including the effect on wage levels and the costs associated with different levels of absenteeism and labour turnover, and the effect on such organisational costs as supervision and maintenance, are all included in this category, as are interest costs and overheads. Such operational consequences have been investigated in a number of work reorganisation experiments, and increasing consideration is being given to assessing them in a more systematic manner, as will be seen below.

Systemic

The consideration of systemic consequences, on the other hand, goes beyond matters of ongoing efficiency to focus on the effect that a work reorganisation programme has on the undertaking's capacity to adapt to the requirements of its environment in the longer term. As such it includes the costs involved in initially committing scarce resources to the reorganisation effort. The costs of additional plant, space and stocks, of covering any initial dip in internal efficiency, and of pursuing the initial, often time-consuming consultations, are included in this category. Conversely the potential benefits to be derived from thus improving the undertaking's over-all ability to respond to changing market and production circumstances are also included in this category, as are the possible advantages of having improved customer relations and, even if over a substantially longer period of time, an organisation more consonant with the changing nature of the social environment. Although the precise economic benefits of such systemic advantages must inevitably remain embodied within over-all financial performance, this should not prevent their separate acknowledgement and consideration: experience is now beginning to suggest that in some cases at least such systemic benefits are real enough.

The way in which more flexible forms of work organisation now improve the responsiveness of production operations to unforeseen market and technological changes has been noted in reports from IBM (Sirota and Wolfson, 1972), Saab (Norstedt and Agurén, 1974), Atlas (Björk, 1975), General Time (Weir, 1976), Pye (Manufacturing Management, 1972) and Volvo (Agurén, Hansson and Karlsson, 1976) amongst many others. The advantages of this kind of work design have been emphasised particularly by enterprises with complex and changing product mixes (Staehle, 1979) and those facing rapidly developing technological environments. Butera (1975, pp. 186-187), in commenting on the experiences of Olivetti, stresses this point:

> To achieve production flexibility, demanded by the increasing complexity of the model mix . . . , the organization had to be such that it would not be necessary to redesign and re-balance the assembly lines every time a variation occurred. The ideal solution was a "cellular" organization that could provide the increase and variety of production merely by adding new organizational units, rather than by making the assembly line longer or shorter.
> Complexity of performance demands and the dynamics of competition make the market life of a product . . . short: . . . What is more, in such a short life cycle, the product does not stay unchanged but undergoes continuous technical modifications, partly stemming from technological evolution and partly from customers' new performance requirements. The time available for implementing a series of operations to simplify, rationalize, and organize the work . . . is therefore extremely limited. This generates a series of temporal and economic restrictions and, as a result, it is no longer feasible to determine a detailed division of labor and work content; the only possible solution is to provide the organizational units and roles with greater autonomy, contrary to the (Taylor) scientific management tradition.

In conditions of discontinuity, which many believe to be more prevalent today, the form of work organisation itself becomes a resource of major importance. Recent research in other areas of management (Burns and Stalker, 1961; Lawrence and Lorsch, 1967) is starting to assess the benefits to be derived from having forms of organisation that can cope with uncertainty and change. Although the benefits may not be quantifiable in precise economic terms, a flexible and responsive organisation of work can undoubtedly contribute to the economic viability of the enterprise as a whole. It is interesting to note that the awareness of such benefits is far from recent. Adam Smith, who did so much to legitimise dominant forms of the division of labour, expressed his own concerns and doubts in the following way:

> In the progress of the division of labour, the employment of the far greater part of those who live by labour, that is, of the great body of the people, comes to be confined to a few very simple operations; frequently to one or two. But the understandings of the greater part of men are . . . formed by their ordinary employments. The man whose life is spent in performing a few simple operations, of which the effects . . . are, perhaps, always the same, or very nearly the same, has no occasion to exert his understanding, or to exercise his invention in finding out expedients for removing difficulties which never occur. He naturally loses, therefore, the habit of such exertion, and generally becomes as stupid and ignorant as it is possible for a human creature to become. . . .
> It is otherwise in the barbarous societies, as they are commonly called, of hunters, of shepherds, and even of husbandmen in that rude state of husbandry which precedes the

119

improvement of manufactures . . . In such societies the varied occupations of every man oblige every man to exert his capacity, and to invent expedients for removing difficulties which are continually occurring. Invention is kept alive, and the mind is not suffered to fall into that drowsy stupidity, which, in a civilised society, seems to benumb the understanding of almost all the inferior ranks of people (Smith, Book V, Chapter 1, Part III, Article II, "Of the expense of the institutions for the education of youth").

Societal

The societal consequences of work organisation are the costs and benefits which, although real and significant, are borne or received by society as a whole rather than by the enterprise from which they emanate. The effects of stress at work on health and on family life (Kornhauser, 1965), for instance, are included in this category, as are the consequences of shift work on the individual and on the cultural life of the community (Mott, 1975) and the wider implications of mechanisation, automation and computerisation themselves and of the patterns of social and work organisation which sustain them. Such societal implications are as diverse as they are profound. Increasing attention is being given to them, particularly in cases in which systemic or operational benefits for the enterprise are clearly associated with societal costs, as when work reorganisation results in lower personnel requirements for the undertaking but higher levels of unemployment in society as a whole. Despite the undoubted and growing importance of societal consequences, and of cases in which there are clear conflicts between social and enterprise objectives, no attempt is made in this paper to review such issues or to consider the evidence to date.

Evidence available

For a more detailed examination of the scope and magnitude of the economic consequences of work organisation at the level of the undertaking consideration must be given to some of the rapidly growing number of reports on individual initiatives and experiments. Regrettably, however, it must be noted that many such reports are not an ideal source of information: there is quite clearly a reporting bias; experiments regarded as being successful have a much higher probability of being the subject of reports available to the public (Cummings and Salipante, 1976), despite the invaluable role that reports of nil and negative results can serve in guiding subsequent endeavours. So any conclusions that may be drawn must be tentative.

In this review two main sources of evidence are considered. First the conclusions of some previous more socially orientated surveys of the published material are presented. Thereafter consideration is given to the more detailed economic effects of a wide variety of work organisation experiments.

General surveys

One of the most systematic analyses of the published results of work reorganisation experiments has been conducted by Srivastva and his colleagues (1975). They identified 57 innovative experiments in which aspects of the work environment had been systematically changed and in which attempts had been made to determine the subsequent effects. An analysis of those experiments revealed that the changes in the work environment had focused on the following nine factors:

(a) pay and reward systems;

(b) autonomy and discretion;

(c) the organisation of support services;

(d) training;

(e) organisational structure;

(f) technology;

(g) task variety;

(h) information and feedback; and

(i) interpersonal and group processes.

Further examination of the experiments revealed, however, that these factors were changed in identifiable combinations. This made it possible to identify four major types of emphasis in work reorganisation:

(1) The establishment of socio-technical groups, work being restructured around self-regulating work groups that performed relatively complete tasks.

(2) The restructuring of jobs, including the expansion of individual jobs both horizontally and vertically.

(3) The introduction of more participation by workers in decisions that directly affected their work lives.

(4) Organisational changes which involved the modification of the formal structure of the organisation and of the information and feedback systems.

On the basis of this classification Srivastva and his colleagues isolated 16 socio-technical experiments, 27 cases of job restructuring, 7 participative management experiments and 7 instances of organisational change.

The analysis considered whether the four types of work reorganisation had a reported positive effect on five outcome factors, namely costs, productivity, quality, withdrawal behaviour, and attitudes. Although the study considered the direction rather than the magnitude of the consequences, it did reveal, as can be seen in table 1, an overwhelming number of positive results in a wide variety of organisational settings, including results that have direct economic consequences: there tended to be improvements in respect of costs, productivity, quality, absenteeism and labour turnover. Both this review and a similar examination of the findings of non-experimental correlation studies of different styles of supervision and work content (Srivastva et al., 1975) forcefully illustrate the potential economic significance of programmes that increase work autonomy, variety and feedback in particular.

Other slightly more comprehensive reviews of work reorganisation experiments have been undertaken, although in a desire to be comprehensive, the authors of such reviews have very often included studies which showed little evidence either of sustained experimentation or of adequate evaluation of its consequences. The mere fact of introducing a change is apparently still regarded as being of some significance. However, another review which deliberately aimed

Table 1. Summary of 57 experimental studies

Particular features	Main thrust of the 57 experiments			
	Establishment of socio-technical or autonomous groups (16 experiments)	Job restructuring (27 experiments)	Participative management (7 experiments)	Organisational change (7 experiments)
Percentage of experiments in which the following features of work organisation were adjusted:				
Pay or reward systems	56	14	. . .	29
Autonomy and discretion	88	92	100	43
Support	31	22	. . .	43
Training	44	33	14	43
Organisational structure	19	14	14	100
Technical and physical conditions	63	22	. . .	29
Task variety	63	79	. . .	14
Information and feedback	63	45	. . .	71
Interpersonal relations or group consciousness	75	4	. . .	43
Results Number of experiments in which results were reported in terms of—				
Costs	8	10	1	2
Productivity	15	20	7	4
Quality	7	17	1	2
Withdrawal behaviour	7	7	5	3
Attitudes	10	21	5	6
Percentage of foregoing cases in which results were wholly positive:				
Costs	88	90	100	50
Productivity	93	75	57	100
Quality	86	100	100	100
Withdrawal behaviour	73	86	80	67
Attitudes	70	76	80	50

Source: S. Srivastva et al.: *Productivity, industrial organization and job satisfaction: Policy developement and implementation,* Report to the National Science Foundation (Case Western Reserve University, 1975).

to exclude cases of the latter kind is reported by Taylor (1977). He found that the vast majority of work organisation experiments were at least reported as being non-negative, and usually as being positive, in their outcomes, although not quite as overwhelmingly positive as those covered in the survey undertaken by Srivastva and his colleagues. The most frequently reported measures of outcome were productivity, output or quantity. The vagueness and diversity of terminology in these and other respects illustrates the difficulties of systematic review and comparison. In 48 per cent of the cases covered some effect on these variables was reported. The second most frequent result was in respect of "job satisfaction", "morale" or just "favourable attitudes", effects on this set of variables being reported in 40 per cent of the cases. Effects on costs were next in order of importance, some improvement, or at least maintenance of cost performance, being reported in 36 per cent of cases. Improvements in quality of output were noted in 20 per cent of the cases and changes in the levels of absenteeism and labour turnover were mentioned in 23 per cent and 17 per cent of the cases respectively. Grievances, safety and accidents, changes in manpower requirements and improved system flexibility were each reported in less than 10 per cent of the cases analysed by Taylor.

The conclusion from this and other surveys (Butteriss and Murdoch, 1975; Butteriss and Murdoch, 1976; Lawler, 1970; Schoderbeck and Rief, 1969; Work in America, 1972) remains that work reorganisation programmes have significant economic potential. Although improvements in job satisfaction and autonomy are important in their own right, their achievement does not stand in isolation. The social and economic aspects of the activities of an enterprise are inextricably intertwined, and work reorganisation can, and often does, improve the economic performance of the enterprise as a whole. For this reason alone the economic dimensions of these experiments would demand specific consideration.

Reports on particular cases

Greater insight into the scope and magnitude of particular economic consequences must come from an examination of some of the rapidly growing number of reports on individual experiments. As has already been noted, these reports are not an ideal source of information. They tend to place much greater emphasis on the human and social consequences of the experiments than on their economic costs and benefits. Indeed in many cases economic data had not been collected at all, and where they had been the reporting was usually far from systematic. Obvious reasons of commercial and industrial relations policy largely account for restrictions on the release of such information; and at least until recently, the publication of economic results has also been restricted by the reluctance of social innovators to be seen as trying to justify social change in economic terms. Despite such problems, however, the reports on individual experiments are useful in two respects. In conjunction they provide a framework for considering the broad range of potential economic consequences: in other words they enable the observer to construct at least a tentative map of the economic linkages that can be affected by changes in the organisation of work. In addition they provide some insight into the potential magnitude of the economic effects; for the latter purpose the individual results, varying as enormously as they do, are less significant than the aggregate picture that is starting to emerge.

Particular costs and benefits

The following discussion of the economic costs and benefits of work reorganisation is first directed to systemic costs, i.e. the initial investment requirements in terms of plant, inventories and training. Thereafter consideration is given to the operational consequences for manpower, materials, output and the over-all efficiency of operations.

Initial investment in plant and machinery

Most of the new forms of work organisation entail higher investment costs for machinery and tools, and for construction costs in the case of new factories designed in accordance with advanced work organisation knowledge.

A number of authorities have estimated that the additional investment in machinery required for doing small-volume assembly work in groups instead of on a flow line is at least 10 per cent for tasks that are labour-intensive and 30 per cent for those that are capital-intensive. In practice the proportion varies enormously, however, depending not only on the specifics of the machinery in question but also on the effect that the reorganisation itself has on machine utilisation. If no improved utilisation is to be expected, investment costs can be at least 50 per cent higher for group and individual working than for line. However, numerous authorities have emphasised the favourable effect that different forms of work organisation can have on the average utilisation of machinery. There is certainly a real possibility of such improved machine utilisation. A recent survey of British experience found that average machine utilisation was only about 50 per cent, with all but 5 per cent of the idle time being the responsibility of management (Midlands Tomorrow, 1975). The fact that new forms of work organisation can capture the potential is demonstrated by at least the early experiences of the Volvo Kalmar plant (Agurén, Hansson and Karlsson, 1976, p. 36) and an experiment in a plastic package manufacturing plant in the United States which resulted in a 50 per cent increase in the actual run time capacity (Taylor et al., 1972).

Similar differences are reflected in the reports of floor space requirements. Generally the establishment of group and individual working places requires greater floor space for machinery, buffer stocks and amenity areas. Additional requirements of between 10 and 25 per cent have been noted for electrical component manufacturing firms (den Hertog, 1976; Manufacturing Management, 1972). For the production of particularly bulky objects, increases of up to 100 per cent at Saab-Scania have been described (Norstedt and Agurén, 1973). In some cases, however, group working can reduce the floor space requirements: in a case of group assembly of typewriters total floor space requirements fell, despite the fact that "social areas" were provided adjacent to each of the reorganised lines (Birchall and Wild, 1974). And in the Langston Company in the United States, manufacturers of heavy machinery for the paper industries, floor space requirements fell by 23 per cent (Williamson, 1972, p. 157). With very few exceptions the additional construction costs of new factories in which all of the latest aspects of job design are incorporated remain shrouded in a great deal of secrecy. It has been estimated, however, that the cost for the Volvo Kalmar plant might be 10 per cent above that of a conventional assembly line plant (Agurén, Hansson and Karlsson, 1976). The additional expenditure in this case was probably the result of the space needed for the group workshop areas and the very generous amenities provided.

Investment in stocks

Again the evidence on the effects of new methods of work organisation on the level of stocks of materials and components is conflicting. The establishment of group and individual working places undoubtedly requires additional stocks (den Hertog, 1976, pp. 90-96), as do less innovative but still modified forms of flow line. However it would appear that this increase in immediate buffer stocks need not result in increases over-all. In large part this is the result of the effect that the new forms of work organisation have on the speed of production.

In many forms of production there is considerable scope for increasing the amount of material processed in a given time (throughput). For batch production, for instance, Williamson (1972, p. 142) estimates that the ratio of actual processing time to total cycle time is unlikely to exceed 1 per cent in many cases, with the high proportion of idle component time resulting in high and costly stocks of work in progress. It was found in a recent British survey of 137 manufacturing plants that the proportion of the production lead time (i.e. the interval between the placing of an order and its delivery) that was spent in processing was less than half in 83 per cent of the plants, and in 45 per cent of them less than a fifth (New, 1976). Moreover, these results related to companies in the flow type industries, in which much higher throughput efficiency can be expected. Although the situation in other countries may be better, it still leaves substantial room for improvement. In the United States, for instance, the proportion of manufacturing plants using less than half the lead time for processing was still 69 per cent in the 1960s (Green, 1970).

It has now been repeatedly demonstrated that different forms of work organisation can improve throughput efficiency and thereby reduce the size of the stocks required: falls of from 25 to 65 per cent in component stocks have been noted in a light engineering works (Kenton, 1973) and of 30 per cent in work in progress at Platt International (Spooner, 1973); the establishment of group working reduced stocks by a factor of six for electron tube assembly at Philips (den Hertog, 1976, p. 112) and by a factor of eight at Ferodo (Williamson, 1972, p. 157). Such differences, and the potential that they point to, suggest that careful planning, estimating and monitoring is required in this respect.

Training and initial consultations

All reports agree that all new forms of work organisation require more money to be spent in training personnel to perform more complex duties. There is also agreement that the additional need for training does not increase in proportion to the complexity of the new task. In the case of Olivetti, for instance, experience suggested that a man "takes considerably less time to learn a whole meaningful job than he does to learn the different factions of the same job" (Butera, 1975, p. 193).

Work reorganisation can also entail a substantial commitment of resources to initial consultations and discussions. These costs include both the cost of external consultants and the use of the time of operating and management personnel. With few exceptions (Mirvis and Macy, 1976), however, these costs are not separately identified, although the exceptions can illustrate their potential magnitude.

Initial dip in productivity

It was found in a survey of experience in Western Europe (Wilkinson, 1970) that an initial commitment of resources was commonly required to cover the fall in productivity that was often an immediate, even if short-term, consequence of work reorganisation. As people learn their new jobs and as the organisation adjusts to the changes, output may fall off at first. But to the extent that the learning is achieved, or the change reinforced, improvements will eventually occur. In a radio assembly plant in the United Kingdom the dip in output lasted from the 10th to the 23rd week of the experiment (Cox and Sharp, 1951).

Wage costs

Owing to the upgrading of tasks, work reorganisation tends to increase the wages of operative workers. There are frequent reports of increases of up to about 10 per cent (Work in America, 1972), some of increases of up to 20 per cent (Taylor, 1977) and a few reports of even higher increases (Butteriss and Murdoch, 1975). The restructuring can also result in higher bonus payments if there are productivity gains and linked incentive payments: reported bonus increases range from 12 to 60 per cent (Donnelly, 1971; Taylor, 1977). In many cases, however, wage costs per unit of production fall because of productivity improvements, and the effect of increases in personnel costs on the cost of products and services is moderated by any effect that the change has on over-all personnel requirements. If it is successful from a management point of view, the reorganisation of work can lead to reductions in operating personnel, and the need for overtime and the use of temporary personnel can also be substantially reduced (British Oxygen Company Ltd., 1971; Kenton, 1973), if not eliminated (Walters, 1975). Direct gains in production efficiency and a reduction in the need to provide for high levels of absenteeism and labour turnover are partly responsible for this, as are the improvements stemming from the higher throughput efficiency that can be derived from group working (New, 1976). When production levels remain more or less static, possibly owing to the state of the market, the absolute number of operating personnel can fall.

Reports note experiments resulting in reductions ranging from 11 to 40 per cent (Butteriss and Murdoch, 1975; Hepworth and Osbaldeston, 1975; Huse and Beer, 1971; Tuggle, 1969; Walton, 1972; Work in America, 1972). With production increases, on the other hand, the personnel savings are reflected in less than proportionate increases in personnel.

Supervisory personnel requirements

The greater autonomy given to working groups can also result in reductions in supervisory personnel. Larger parts of the tasks of assigning work, training new employees, administering materials and checking on production quality tend to be done by the operating personnel themselves. Supervision was reduced, for example, by 50 per cent after the introduction of semi-autonomous working groups in a plastic package manufacturing plant in the United States (Taylor et al., 1972). Group working in aircraft maintenance at Air Canada (Chartrand, 1976) resulted in reductions of up to 75 per cent in supervision time. A job enlargement scheme in an engineering department of the American Telephone and Telegraph company reduced the number of management jobs at various levels and produced cost savings of $250,000 annually (Taylor, 1977). Similar results have been reported for Volvo (Agurén, Hansson and Karlsson, 1976) and Imperial Chemical Industries (Cotgrove, Dunham and Vamplew, 1971).

Furthermore the combination of quality improvements and the relocation of the inspection function within the work group can result in large reductions in quality and other control personnel. In the United Kingdom side of the Shell firm, testing in one department fell by 75 per cent (Hill, 1972). A work reorganisation programme in the quality control function of an International Business Machines plant in the United States resulted in a 50 per cent reduction in inspection, with the number of inspectors falling from 48 to 28 (Mahel, Overbagh, Palmer and Piersol, 1970).

Absenteeism and labour turnover

There are innumerable reports of work reorganisation programmes resulting in lower absenteeism and labour turnover (Locke, 1976). Until recently, however, there have been very few attempts to estimate the resulting economic gains. The difficulties are great: even the concepts of absenteeism, and especially labour turnover, are imprecise and subject to varying definitions and forms of statistical calculation (Latham and Pursell, 1975; Price, 1973; Van der Merwe and Miller, 1971). Yet even if some of the all too real societal consequences are ignored, reductions in absenteeism and labour turnover can clearly offer direct economic benefits to an enterprise, for recruiting costs are real enough. Personnel department costs can be affected directly and economic gains will certainly accrue if losses in production can be prevented, overtime working reduced and manpower requirements cut. Moreover high levels of absenteeism and labour turnover can jeopardise the productive capacity of a whole group of workers. These consequences have long been recognised, and in many cases have provided the impetus for organisational change; but few attempts have been made to calculate them precisely.

An early impetus for many of the endeavours to quantify the economic consequences of various forms of withdrawal behaviour was provided by Likert (1967). His plea for "human resource accounting" captured the imagination and energies of a small but enthusiastic group of scholars and practioners. A great deal of theoretical and practical development has been undertaken since that time (Flamholtz, 1974) and, if used with care, some of the ideas that have been developed might provide some guidelines for action. Working with insurance company employees, for instance, Flamholtz estimated that the replacement costs for claims personnel ranged from US$6,000 for a claims investigator to US$24,000 for a field examiner and those for sales personnel from US$31,600 for salesmen with below-average performance to US$185,100 for a sales manager.

Unfortunately, however, a great deal of the work on human resource accounting has been more notable for its technical sophistication than for its relationship to management concerns. Yet in one company human resource accounting information was used to identify the total investment cost of changing an assembly operation from flow-line to group working. Estimates made of the orientation, training, familiarisation and dislocation costs demonstrated that the "human resource costs" of the change-over amounted to almost four times the physical capital cost (Woodruff, 1974, pp. 16-17). And in the light of this surprising finding the company developed and used a regular financial report on human resources costs for management purposes.

Research and development work on more systematic methods of costing the consequences of personnel turnover is currently in progress in a number of organisations (Gustafson, 1974; Jonson, Jönsson and Svenson, 1979). Moreover, to assess the economic benefits of reductions in absenteeism and labour turnover stemming from programmes designed to improve the quality of working life, Herrick (1975) and more particularly Macy and Mirvis (1976) are developing methodologies suitable for more general application. This approach relies on an intensive analysis of the range of possible organisational responses to absenteeism and labour turnover, and of their financial implications in terms of direct, indirect and opportunity costs. The accompanying figure illustrates how the responses to absenteeism were mapped and costed. Using this approach Macy and Mirvis found that the average cost of one day's absenteeism in an assembly plant in the United States was $55.36 in 1972-73, including downtime costs of $10.03, fringe benefits paid to the missing employee of $5.12, replacement workforce costs of $6.29 and under-absorbed fixed costs of $33.92. The average cost per "incident of turnover" was $120.59 in 1972-73, rising to $150.69 in 1974-75. These methods can be criticised for the assumptions they make, the methods they employ (under-absorbed overheads indeed!), their complexity of calculation and their pseudo-precision; but they should not be dismissed out of hand: at the very least they emphasise the potential management significance of the economic consequences of withdrawal behaviour and, in so doing, the inadequacies of traditional accounting methods.

While research in this field proceeds, management should not ignore the issue. The crude estimates of economic effect now being used by a few companies (Taylor, 1973; Weir, 1976) might well be preferable to ignoring the real effects that absenteeism and labour turnover can have on the financial and social performance of the enterprise.

Quality of output and reduction of waste

Many attempts to reorganise the working environment have resulted in an improvement in the quality of the work done. Scrap, reject and error rates have fallen. Rejects, for instance, fell by 80 per cent as a result of an autonomous working group design at the Topeka plant of General Foods (Work in America, 1972); Philips have reported falls of from 9 to 5 per cent and from 7 to 3 per cent in rejects (den Hertog, 1974; Jenkins, 1974); and in a continuous weld pipe mill in California, group working resulted in a fall from 39 to 9 per cent in spoilage. Several companies have by now estimated the economic advantages of these improvements. A simple approach involving estimates of the cost of scrap, customer returns and re-work, and the gains from recoveries, is outlined by Macy and Mirvis (1976).

Similar improvements have also been found with clerical jobs. Job enrichment at Imperial Chemical Industries resulted in reports of higher quality (Paul and Robertson, 1970), and the use of self-governing work groups in the motor

128

Measuring the costs of absenteeism

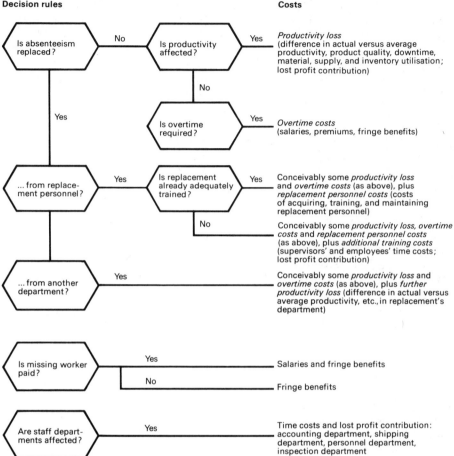

(Source: Barry A. Macy and Philip H. Mirvis: "A methodology for assessment of quality of work life and organizational effectiveness in behavioral-economic terms", in *Administrative Science Quarterly*, June 1976, p. 226.)

insurance office at Skandia cut the number of misplaced documents from 1,200 to 7 in the first four months of the new system (Hepworth and Osbaldeston, 1975). A more controlled experiment in the accounting office of a United States insurance company found that group work resulted in a fall in error rates of 35 per cent by comparison with returns from a control group (Ulich, 1974). Such gains are unlikely to be amenable to economic assessment, however.

It would appear that improvements in quality have been achieved principally where an individual or a group has taken responsibility for quality control. An increased sense of responsibility is, in part, responsible for the findings, although the clearer delineation of responsibility and the shorter feedback time also promotes more learning on the job.

Organisational costs

Work reorganisation programmes can also affect the overhead or organisational costs of an enterprise. As a result of the reduction in supervisory and control personnel there can be other related cost reductions. The introduction of autonomous working groups in Proctor and Gamble's Lima, Ohio, processing plant resulted, for instance, in falls of from 10 to 50 per cent in a wide variety of overhead costs (Jenkins, 1973). There can also be cost reductions stemming from the higher safety standards that can, on occasions, be associated with new forms of work organisation. Macy and Mirvis (1976) present a tentative way of gaining some insight into the possible immediate economic implications of such standards. Maintenance costs can also be affected, positively or negatively: on the one hand the shift of some maintenance functions to a group, and their increased responsibility for the plant in their care, can result in maintenance cost reductions; however, to the extent that the reorganisation results in a need for more production equipment, maintenance costs can increase. Evidence varies on this point.

Over-all operational efficiency of resource utilisation

The foregoing discussion has reflected the rather fragmented nature of evaluative efforts. Emphasis has been placed on particular costs and benefits. Taken individually they tend to give a rather narrow and partial view of the effect of work reorganisation programmes, although in conjunction they do provide an indication of the broad range of potential over-all economic consequences. However, the assessment of over-all efficiency is notoriously difficult. Nevertheless, it has attracted the interest of many scholars and practitioners over many decades. The reasons for this are clear enough. In the undertaking a diversity of resources are employed in the production of a common group of products and services. Although it is useful for management to have indicators of the performance of separate resources at its disposal, it is also desirable that it should have some indication of their joint operation. However, the rationale for having indicators of over-all efficiency itself indicates their limitations. The problems of equating diverse resources are real (Salter, 1969), and even if they are surmounted the making of comparisons across enterprises, and even across functions and departments within a single enterprise, can be a difficult if not impossible task.

Productivity and throughput, the two common measures of over-all results, can provide useful, albeit crude, indicators of the immediate effect of work reorganisation programmes, and they are used for that purpose in numerous reports. However, such measurements need to be used with care. They give only a partial reflection of many of the economic gains derived from organisational changes, and fail to reflect many of the longer-term benefits. Also, as commonly defined, they do not enable any distinction to be made between the returns to the social reorganisation of work itself and to the higher capital investment which often accompanies such reorganisation. Some effort has been devoted to isolating the contributions of separate factors. The French research and experimentation on surplus accounts is particularly interesting in this respect (Lemaine, 1977;

Maître, 1979; and Templé, 1971). On the other hand, some authorities might now see the crudeness of productivity and throughput indicators as a potential advantage, focusing the attention of the observer on the over-all result instead of on the contributions of separate factors. In short, such over-all indicators of performance are useful, and throughput measurements, in particular, help to emphasise the relevance of time. But as means of assessing the economic consequences of a work reorganisation programme they cannot and should not stand on their own. Whilst they reflect in a simple manner some aspects of the over-all balance of gains and losses, and in so doing relate to the routine measurements of operational performance made in many enterprises, other vital consequences are ignored. Accordingly they can, with care, be used to supplement a consideration of the full range of economic consequences, but not as a substitute for it.

Fortunately some of the more recent attempts to move towards more comprehensive assessment have borne such considerations in mind. An instance is the economic assessment of the group technology programme introduced by Serck Audco Valves Ltd., manufacturers of taper plug valves (Williamson, 1972). In the early 1960s Serck Audco had experienced difficulties in meeting delivery dates on export orders. An examination of the flow of products through the manufacturing process showed that the traditional methods of production were resulting in materials spending an average of 80 per cent of their total time in the factory in queues waiting for the completion of other components and the necessary adjustment and resetting of the machine tools. In the light of this examination the company developed the idea of cellular manufacture, a comprehensive socio-technical approach to the organisation of work which involved every function of the company (see Vol. 1 of the present publication, pp. 117-121). Between 1961-62 and 1966-67 the manufacturing time for products declined from 12 weeks to two-and-a-half. This contributed to a 44 per cent reduction in stocks during the same period and a consequent fall in the ratio of stocks to sales from 52 to 22 per cent. Indeed the initial capital invested in the conversion to group technology was recovered four times over by the stock reduction alone.

Recently a number of attempts have been made to provide a more comprehensive assessment of programmes designed to improve the quality of working life in both social and economic terms. The recent reports on the Volvo Kalmar plant made by Volvo itself and the Swedish Rationalisation Council (Agurén, Hansson and Karlsson, 1976) are indicative of the trend, as are the economic and social evaluations conducted elsewhere by Volvo and by Philips (den Hertog, 1976; Jonson, Jönsson and Svensson, 1979). The outline of the approach used by Saab-Scania has also been published (Norstedt and Agurén, 1973, pp. 39-40). Numerous other assessments of varying detail, scope and sophistication are being made, although few are available to the public.

By far the most comprehensive approach to assessment to date is contained in the work of Herrick (1975) and Macy and Mirvis (1976). The latter authors in particular are developing and applying a social and economic methodology for defining, measuring and costing the forms of behaviour on the job that are likely to be influenced by the reorganisation of work. These authors provide three criteria for the inclusion of a form of behaviour in their measurement scheme:

(a) it has to be defined so that it is significantly affected by the work structure;

(b) it has to be measurable and convertible to significant costs to the organisation; and

(c) the measures and costs of the behaviour variables have to be mutually exclusive.

On these bases the emergent methodology focuses on determining the economic and social consequences of ten types of variables in two broad categories, namely participation and membership behaviour (e.g. absenteeism, labour turnover and strikes) and job performance behaviour (e.g. production under standard, grievances, quality under standard, accidents, unscheduled downtime and machine repair, and material utilisation and inventory shrinkage). In all cases the standard measures of the costs of these variables were derived from accepted organisational and accounting practice. Distinctions were made between initial outlay costs and time costs, and also between variable or direct costs, fixed or indirect costs and the opportunity costs associated with lost potential. The approach has now been used to assess the costs and benefits of a number of work reorganisation programmes. An example based on experience in a manufacturing and assembly plant is illustrated in tables 2 and 3. Table 2 reports the cost per incident and the total estimated organisational costs for each variable at the site during the baseline period (1972-73) and the first two stages of the reorganisation. These figures are cast into a cost-benefit framework in table 3, where the costs of the reorganisation programme are compared with the year-to-year changes in the cost of counter-productive behaviour. In this instance the over-all outcome at the end of the whole biennium remains negative. The total direct costs of $303,588 are associated with an indirect cost of $227,240, giving an over-all economic cost of $530,828.

However, measurement problems abound, and the organisational relevance and social implications of such comprehensive approaches to evaluation have still to be assessed. However, these approaches should not be ignored, since they do, at the very least, reflect a sincere desire to learn and inform. Although existing approaches are bound to be superseded in the course of the advancement of knowledge (see, for example, the ongoing work of Epple, Fidler and Goodman), the early efforts indicate an emerging desire to integrate social and economic forms of assessment, so that they can together provide a basis for more detailed and specific knowledge of the organisation of work.

Some influences on the economic effects of the reorganisation of work

The review of the detailed reports of particular operational consequences stemming from work reorganisation programmes, together with the earlier discussion of the possibilities for achieving real systemic gains, points to the economic potential of organisational changes of this type at the level of the undertaking. It would appear that they can indeed generate as well as consume economic resources, as traditionally defined, and so contribute to the economic

Table 2. Estimated costs of various aspects of worker behaviour at a plant in the United States, 1972-75 (In US dollars)

Type of incident	1972-73		1973-74		1974-75[1]	
	Cost per incident	Total cost	Cost per incident	Total cost	Cost per incident	Total cost
Absenteeism[2]						
Leave days	...		55.04	687 229	61.64	821 795
Other	55.36	286 360	53.15	510 453	62.49	431 494
Accidents[2]						
Reportable[3]	727.39	194 213	698.31	229 046	1 106.52	240 115
Minor[3]	6.64	21 122	5.71	38 331	6.45	35 856
Re-visits to plant first-aid facilities	6.64	11 992	5.71	14 018	6.45	13 081
Late arrival at work[2,4]	4.86	56 920	...	...	...	...
Labour turnover (cessations of employment)[2]						
Voluntary resignation	120.59	18 089	131.68	33 973	150.69	18 083
Other	120.59	14 230	131.68	21 859	150.69	18 686
Submission of grievance[5]	32.48	1 851	34.44	1 378	56.10	2 300
Product quality below standard[6]	19 517	663 589	19 517	573 800	19 517	409 857
Labour productivity below standard[7]	22 236	266 838	22 236	335 764	22 236	255 714
Totals[8,9]		1 535 204		2 445 851		2 246 971

[1] Costs associated with absenteeism, accidents, labour turnover and grievances during the last four months of this year are projections. The figures for product quality and labour productivity below standard are actual costs. [2] Rates and costs for salaried personnel are assumed to be the same as those for hourly paid workers (1972-73: salaried absence costs, $41,669; salaried accident costs, $11,638; salary costs of late arrivals, $9,641; salaried labour turnover costs, $1,829). [3] Under Section 8(c)(2) of the Occupational Safety and Health Act of 1970 (ILO: Legislative Series, 1970—USA 1), the Secretary of Labor, in co-operation with the Secretary of Health, Education, and Welfare, issues regulations requiring employers to report on "work-related deaths, injuries and illnesses other than minor injuries requiring only first-aid treatment and which do not involve medical treatment, loss of consciousness, restriction of work or motion, or transfer to another job". [4] The "tardiness" concept measured here in fact covered each absence or illness lasting less than 4 hours; the average was 27 minutes. [5] In writing in accordance with the labour-management contract. [6] For 1972-73 the costs of rejects and scrap was 3.4 per cent of total sales. Each reduction of 1 per thousand is valued at $19,517 per incident. In 1973-74 costs were 2.94 per cent of total sales; in 1974-75, 2.1 per cent. A constant dollar equivalence of $19,517 was used in 1973-74 and 1974-75 to discount inflation. The non-discounted cost of quality below standard in 1973-74 was $667,015 ($23,028 per incident); in 1974-75 the non-discounted cost was $613,970 ($29,237 per incident). [7] In 1972-73 plant productivity was 88 per cent of standard. The production below standard rate is 12 per cent; accordingly a reduction of 1 per cent is valued at $22,236 per incident. Plant productivity in 1973-74 and 1974-75 was 84.9 per cent and 88.5 per cent of standard respectively. A constant dollar equivalence of $22,236 was used to discount inflation in 1973-74 and 1974-75. The non-discounted cost of production below standard was $400,567 ($26,528 per incident) in 1973-74 and $290,938 ($25,299 per incident) in 1974-75. [8] The total cost in 1972-73 is $1,470,427 for hourly paid personnel, and $64,777 for salaried personnel. [9] The total cost is reflected in standard labour dollars. The estimated cost in real dollar equivalents in 1972-73: $1,688,724, or 10.4 per cent of sales; in 1973-74: $2,690,436, or 8.45 per cent of sales; in 1974-75: $2,471,668, or 10.61 per cent of sales.

Source: Barry A. Macy and Philip H. Mirvis: "A methodology for assessment of quality of work life and organizational effectiveness in behavioural-economic terms", in *Administrative Science Quarterly*, June 1976, p. 219.

Table 3. Financial cost-benefit analysis of a human resource development project at a plant
in the United States, 1973-75
(In US dollars; differences from base year 1972-73)

Item	Initial year (May 1973-April 1974)	Second year (May 1974-April 1975)	Whole biennium
Direct costs			
Consultant fees, expenses, etc.[1]	225 000	61 600	
Site employee time, training activities, earned idle time, etc.[2]	2 403	14 585	
Totals	227 403	76 185	303 588
Indirect benefits (or costs)[3]			
Absenteeism	(224 093)	(145 134)	
Leave days	. . .	. . .	
Accidents			
Reportable	(34 833)	(45 902)	
Minor	(17 209)	(14 734)	
Re-visits	(2 026)	(1 089)	
Late arrival at work	. . .	. . .	
Labour turnover (cessations of employment)			
Voluntary resignation	(15 884)	6	
Other	(7 629)	(4 456)	
Submission of grievances	473	(449)	
Product quality in relation to standard	89 789	253 732	
Labour productivity in relation to standard	(68 926)	11 124	
Totals	(280 338)	53 098	(227 240)

[1] Nine different organisations and funding agencies made financial contributions to the project. In addition, three organisations provided office space and services. These contributions are excluded from the analysis. [2] Estimates of actual costs are low because only personnel paid by the hour are included. [3] For definitions see table 2, from which all estimates of indirect benefits or costs are derived.

and social vitality of the enterprise. Of course such potential is not always achieved. Regardless of the difficulties of recording and monitoring accomplishment, particular experiments can fail to exploit the full possibilities that are seemingly available and others, although initially achieving some positive economic results, do not maintain them over time.

The reasons for such failures are many and complex. The nature of the change process itself is often an important factor, as are the precise mode of implementation, the implications of the change for the structure of power and influence in the organisation and the congruity or otherwise of the change with the social values and norms prevailing in the enterprise. But whilst undoubtedly important, the roles that might be played by such social and organisational factors are discussed elsewhere (Davis and Cherns, 1975; and particularly Mirvis and Berg, 1978). Here, emphasis will be placed on the way in which the framework for considering the economic costs and benefits of work reorganisation programmes that has been outlined above can help to identify some further factors that can influence the over-all economic effect of a change programme.

An analysis of the framework points to the ways in which a number of structural characteristics of the undertaking can influence the extent to which the social implications of an organisational change programme affect its over-all economic results. The capital intensity of the enterprise, for instance, is capable of influencing both the level of the initial systemic costs for a programme of work reorganisation and at least some elements of operational advantage. The capital investment needed to bring about a change can often be high, but for a capital-intensive enterprise the benefits stemming from higher throughput, and particularly those associated with reductions in absenteeism and turnover, can be correspondingly great. Not only can many of the costs of lost production time be avoided, but the undertaking can also gain from greater flexibility of operation.

Similarly an economic perspective highlights the relevance of considering the cost structure of the product or service. That structure provides the weights for assessing the relative economic significance of any operational costs and benefits in the fields of personnel, material and organisational (or overhead) costs (New, 1976). For example, the costs of producing products or services with a low added value will be lowered by work reorganisation programmes which result in gains on the utilisation of materials; products or services with a high personnel content will more readily benefit economically from programmes that result in reduced labour requirements or substantial improvements with regard to absenteeism or labour turnover; and enterprises with high organisational complexity, having a great deal of vertical and horizontal differentiation of tasks, have greater opportunities to reduce the resources devoted to supervision and other forms of hierarchical control.

Other things being equal, product models or particular services that are produced for a longer period also offer greater possibilities for reaping the potential benefits of work reorganisation programmes, for the longer the period the greater is the likelihood of achieving a positive ratio of the operational benefits gained to the initial investment of resources. Moreover, the sooner work is reorganised during the period of production of a particular model or service, the greater the economic benefits (den Hertog, 1976, pp. 147-148). It should be borne in mind in this connection that new forms of work organisation can reduce the costs incurred by an enterprise as it seeks to adjust to the shorter model lives that are a characteristic of the modern industrial era, as was illustrated by the experience of Olivetti discussed above (Butera, 1975). For by comparison with enterprises operating in a stable environment, those that have to cope with continuing uncertainty can gain more from the systemic benefits that can stem from more flexible forms of work organisation. Indeed the experience of Bosch and Siemens (Staehle, 1974), Olivetti (Butera, 1975) and others illustrates how the desire to reap the potential systemic benefits of different forms of work organisation can itself promote change.

At this stage in the development of knowledge of the economic consequences of programmes designed to improve the quality of working life it might be useful to pay special attention to such structural factors as the capital intensity of the enterprise, its organisational complexity, the length of model life, the uncertainty of the task environment and the market, and the cost structure of the product or service. It might be admitted that the factors listed are not the basic ones. The technological environment of an undertaking, for instance, may be a major determinant of many economic consequences; but factors such as these do have the advantage of providing a pragmatic way of considering in broad terms the over-all significance of the many separate economic effects.

Performance of different forms of organisation

The emerging interest in the economic effectiveness of more radically different forms of organisation and management may also afford some insight into the economic viability of new approaches to work organisation. Co-operative and self-managed undertakings certainly have many characteristics that go beyond the changes envisaged in the designs for most programmes aiming to improve the quality of working life in conventionally managed enterprises. On the other hand some of the objectives are not dissimilar, nor are some of the means through which they are achieved.

Melman's study of the comparative performance of traditionally managed undertakings and co-operative societies in Israel is interesting in this respect (Melman, 1970-71). Comparing a paired sample of enterprises in the tool, instruments, diecasting, plastics, machining and canning industries, he found that over-all the co-operative societies showed higher labour productivity (26 per cent), higher capital productivity (67 per cent), larger net profit per production worker (115 per cent) and lower administrative costs (13 per cent). Certainly the more democratic mode of decision-making in these co-operative undertakings was at least as efficient, and probably more efficient, than the more hierarchical forms of decision-making practised in a comparable set of managerially controlled firms.

An even more relevant study was based on a comparison of productivity in worker-managed and conventional firms in the United States plywood industry (Berman, 1976). The opportunity to make this comparison revolves around several intriguing court cases in the United States that sought to determine whether co-operative societies pay higher wages (which are not taxed as company profits). In one case a co-operative society producing plywood in the North-West was able to satisfy the courts that one hour of its members' time was worth 30 to 50 per cent more than that of workers doing the same work in conventional firms. After ensuing audits of several other undertakings, the United States tax authorities have accepted the 30 per cent higher productivity figure as valid. The studies undertaken by consultants on behalf of the tax authorities demonstrated that the higher productivity in the co-operative societies was due to the fact that they had fewer foremen, that workers maintained their own machinery and that the members learned more jobs and were thus able to rotate jobs when needed. In many cases the workers also performed what elsewhere would be classified as executive-level jobs without additional pay. According to the author of the report the higher performance in the co-operative societies was due to the fact that they had used many of the approaches that are now being explored by conventional firms, such as autonomous working groups, participative approaches to decision-making and a greater disclosure of information.

As yet, the results of such studies are only indicative. They suggest, however, that a more detailed consideration of the economic performance of different forms of management might be able to provide some further insights into the potential of new forms of work organisation. Some other intriguing evidence on the economic aspects of work organisation is provided by studies conducted on comparable firms in France and the Federal Republic of Germany collected by the Laboratoire d'Economie et de Sociologie du Travail at Aix-en-Provence (Brossard and Maurice, 1976; Lutz, 1976; and also Fitzroy and Hiller, 1978). French firms appeared to be more stratified, hierarchical and centralised. The administrative workforce was larger and better paid at higher levels in France, while production workers were better trained and paid in the Federal Republic, where the division of labour was less pronounced and screening by formal education less prevalent. More recent research puts the United Kingdom in an intermediary position (Maurice, Sorge and Warner, 1978). Such results at least point to the practical possibility of theoretical options, particularly since the firms in France and the Federal Republic of Germany, at least, appeared to be similar in respect of their profitability and total labour costs.

Future possibilities and needs

The foregoing review of past experience and insights has amply illustrated the economic potential of programmes designed to improve the quality of working life. It would appear that although directed to social ends, such programmes not only consume economic resources but can create further economic resources and add to the longer-term economic and social viability of the enterprise. When seen in these terms, the need for economic and social assessment is real enough: a great deal of fundamental and, in the best sense of the word, challenging experimentation is needed in this field. In the meantime, however, the subject cannot and should not be ignored. Enterprises trying to reorganise their work environment should be encouraged to concern themselves with the economic and the social consequences of so doing.

Much of the information required for any such analysis can be obtained without too much difficulty from existing accounting systems. Certainly the necessary information on the initial costs of a work reorganisation programme can be obtained in this way. Details of changing requirements for both operational and supervisory personnel, and the associated costs, will be an integral part of any standard accounting system. So will details of the changing investment in stocks and work in progress and the effect on organisational costs and overheads. A good indication of the benefits of improved product quality can be obtained from savings on the costs of scrap, customer returns and re-working. The only difficulty in all of these cases is to compile and present the information in a way that emphasises the effect of a programme, is instructive, and provides a basis for decision. Past experience in this and other fields of accounting suggests, however, that it will not be easy to meet these requirements. In addition, there are major difficulties in two particular fields. The first relates to the assessment of economic costs and benefits in service and clerical organisations, in which accounting systems are generally not so well developed. Although most such systems should give a useful indication of initial costs, changing personnel costs and the effects on organisational overheads, there will be enormous and in most cases insurmountable problems in estimating the economic implications of work of higher quality. If those implications are considered important, it will usually be necessary to rely on broad indicators of the changing nature of the task rather than on precise economic calculations.

The other exceptionally difficult task is the assessment of the economic consequences of changes in such matters as grievances, absenteeism, labour turnover and accidents and the calculation of the longer-term systemic benefits that were outlined above. However difficult it may be, some effort should be made to calculate these more subtle economic implications of an improved work environment, to which in many cases the major benefits may be due. Lower absenteeism and labour turnover, for instance, can contribute to the financial performance of an enterprise. Productivity losses can be prevented, overtime and the use of temporary personnel can be reduced, savings can be made in the organisational costs associated with replacement, and on occasion over-all personnel requirements can be cut. It is common knowledge that traditional accounting systems are not designed to provide a ready assessment of such gains. The necessary data are in many cases collected but then lost in the mass of calculations which give rise to the measurement of over-all financial performance. With imagination and perseverance, however, what has been so lost can often be found. A few enterprises are now starting to demonstrate that such estimates can be made. Absenteeism is being related to lost production and overtime. Similar estimates of productivity losses, higher personnel costs and the often high costs of replacement are being related to labour turnover. Whilst often imprecise and partial, such indicators can be useful. Even if only collected irregularly, they can highlight the significant relationship between the social and the economic environment of the enterprise. The more sophisticated endeavours of Herrick (1975) and Macy and Mirvis (1976) may not, at this stage, be suitable for general use. But they do suggest the need for more practical but rigorous research in this field, and indicate its potential.

When the economic consequences of programmes designed to improve the quality of working life are being evaluated, primary emphasis should be placed on examining the over-all costs and benefits of a programme rather than on calculating ratios merely of productive performance and efficiency. Such ratios have their uses, but they can give only a partial and short-term indication of the over-all effect. To be instructive and provide an adequate basis for action, a delineation and assessment of systemic and operational costs and benefits must involve the computation and analysis of a whole range of indicators. Only in this way can the more subtle long-term influences of work reorganisation programmes be recognised and considered. Consideration should be given in particular to placing greater emphasis on the concept of value added (sales less purchases of raw materials and supplies) when reporting on both the over-all consequences of work reorganisation programmes and their particular effect on productivity ratios. By comparison with other indicators of financial performance, value added is particularly dependent on the joint role that capital and labour play in the creation of wealth. Without lending support to the assumption that the use of some resources, such as labour, gives rise to "costs" whilst others, such as capital, are properly rewarded by the distribution of profit, the calculation of value added focuses attention on the proportion of the total wealth created in the enterprise not only by the different parties but also over time. Wages and salaries, interest and dividends, and taxes can, in that way, be compared with the resources that have been set aside for ensuring the longer-term existence, viability and growth of the enterprise.

Unless special care is taken, economic assessments can all too readily focus attention on the calculation of short-term gains rather than longer-term systemic benefits. Hence consideration needs to be given to the joint use of social and economic indicators that can help to suggest whether programmes designed to improve the quality of working life are or are not giving rise to the systemic benefits discussed above. The aim should be to consider not the partial or immediate effect of a programme but its over-all long-term effect. An initial investment might have to be made in work in progress and raw material stocks, for instance, to provide buffers for group and individual working. In time, however, if a reorganisation programme has a favourable effect on throughput, these investments may pay for themselves. Similarly, many reorganisation programmes result in a higher wage and salary bill. Again, however, if a programme improves productivity, the personnel component of product costs will not increase in the same proportion. Care should be taken to include estimates of the initial dip in productivity when calculating the initial costs of a programme. The costs associated with consultation and training should also be included. In many cases these can be as high as the costs of physical capital and inventories, if not higher (Woodruff, 1974). However, even higher costs of training for each worker need not necessarily result in higher total training costs. Volkswagen, for example, found that the lower rate of labour turnover resulting from a work reorganisation programme led to a reduction in the total cost of training new workers (Lindestad and Kvist, 1975). Numerous other instances of such secondary effects could be cited. However, the foregoing examples are sufficient to explain why an attempt should be made to cover secondary effects when assessing economic consequences.

The broad approach to the assessment of economic costs and benefits that has been outlined above aims to be useful and convenient. In most respects it should be relatively easy to follow in most undertakings. Matters such as the effects of "withdrawal behaviour" (absenteeism and high labour turnover) and longer-term systemic benefits are more difficult to handle. They should not be forgotten, however. There is a need for pragmatic experimentation in enterprises with the aim of producing a range of convenient, short-term solutions, and facilities for the exchange of experience in this respect could usefully be established. At the same time, more fundamental research should be encouraged with the objective of producing acceptable, usable and low cost means of long-term assessment.

Organisational role of economic assessment

In trying to assess economic consequences consideration must be given to the process by which the indicators are designed. For it would be paradoxical indeed if methods of economic measurement were applied without discrimination to a new social and technological structure the very existence of which may reflect broader conceptions of the social nature of the design process. With few exceptions, however, recommendations for new methods of economic assessment tend to be designed either by a small group of internal specialists or by outside consultants (Edstrom, 1976; Powers, 1972; Swanson, 1974). The designers invariably try to follow a path of seeming technical objectivity, appealing to the "obvious" needs of the enterprise "as a whole". But in so doing they often ignore many of the wider organisational factors that determine the potential use and final effect of their recommendations. This state of affairs may well explain present apprehensions and lack of progress in the economic assessment of new forms of work organisation.

Specialist skills are undeniably needed in designing means of economic assessment, but it should always be remembered that the method finally adopted reflects social as well as economic values. At the very least the specification of the organisational purpose to be served and the principles that should govern the design and use of the method should be discussed and challenged by a wider circle. Wherever possible, the whole design process should be on a participatory basis, for if that is not done new methods of work organisation will be assessed on the basis of procedures that neglect the fundamental tenets of what they are supposed to assess.

Most discussions of economic assessment tend to emphasis the technical aspects of evaluative methodologies rather than the organisational purposes which they can serve and the context in which they are to be used. Yet broader organisational issues can play a key role in determining not only whether a methodology is accepted and used but also the precise nature of its effect on decisions and action. Indeed many of the most difficult problems in the assessment of the economic costs and benefits of new approaches to work organisation are likely to result from apprehensions and anxieties over the context in which such an assessment will be used and the purpose it will serve. Will the new approaches be used, like so many other information and assessment systems, to support existing structures of hierarchical control? Or can they encourage a wider organisational interest and involvement in the possibilities and effects of change? Who, in other words, will be able to use the new calculations rather than be subjected to them? And are they truly capable of helping to change people's outlook, as some of their advocates claim? Or might they merely bring about greater organisational rigidity as people strive to satisfy their more immediate requirements rather than the broader ends which are the proclaimed intention of the designers?

A concern with further economic assessment can also engender anxieties because it can be seen as implying, albeit in a disguised form, a challenge to the value of social progress. Galbraith (1974, p. 7) notes that the "contribution of economics to the exercise of power . . . [is] instrumental in that it serves not the understanding or improvement of the economic system but the goals of those who have power in the system". However, although the stereotype of the "dismal science" can all too readily encourage a concern with the visible hand of economic restraint, in the present context it is important to state that such a concern is not necessarily justified. All depends on the context in which the information is used.

Whilst the distinction between economic and social assessment has its uses, it should not be carried too far. There are few social ends that do not require the use of economic resources, and economic progress, in turn, can often create significant social change. Instead of continuing to enforce an artificial distinction between the social and the economic, progress requires "the development of a comprehensive set of criteria that will take account of both economic and social considerations, not by forcing the one into the mould of the other, but by integrating them at a higher level of abstraction" (United Nations, 1965, p. 10). Assessment is always a complex social as well as technical activity. The organisational roles which it can and does serve extend well beyond those that are used to justify it. Although some of these roles may not be readily acknowledged by the organisations themselves, they can none the less exert influence on the acceptance and use of new approaches. Accordingly, change in this respect must of necessity be seen as a difficult and demanding activity. Instead of being ignored, the organisational and social dimensions increasingly need to be seen as an essential part of the whole problem of bringing about change.

Conclusion

This survey has shown that new forms of work organisation and programmes designed to improve the quality of working life can make a positive contribution to the over-all economic performance of an organisation. They are often costly, but the resulting benefits can not only improve operational functioning but also contribute to an organisation's capacity to adjust to changing needs and circumstances. Longer-term systemic gains can, in other words, often supplement the more visible operational savings in personnel, material and organisational costs.

Many troublesome measurement problems remain, however. Although much can be learnt from an informed use of existing flows of enterprise-level financial information, that information is usually collected to serve a particular purpose of the organisation itself rather than to shed light on the possible need for a change in the form of the organisation of work. So many social assumptions underlie the prevailing forms of evaluation that invariably more tends to be known about current effects of new forms of work organisation than about their possible value in the longer term. However, as social values continue to change and as society's conceptions of the social nature and roles of the enterprise evolve along with them, more attention is being devoted to methods of economic assessment and appraisal. Although current approaches to social accounting and social audit may be crude and embryonic, they are nevertheless significant reflections of our changing conceptions of the accountability of the enterprise. Greater attention also is being paid to the interests of labour: not only has there been an increasing concern with the problems of disclosing information to workers and trade unions, but all over Europe interest is now being expressed in broader definitions of economic surplus and in forms of reporting that give different accounts of workplace behaviour and achievements. Such developments could have major implications for the economic assessment of programmes designed to improve the quality of working life. If they do succeed in challenging prevailing notions of enterprise performance, the current searchings and experiments may provide the basis for a broader and more vital portrayal of life in the enterprise as a whole.

References

Agurén, Stefán; Hansson, Reine; and Karlsson, K. G. *The Volvo Kalmar plant: The impact of new design on work organization.* Stockholm, Rationalization Council SAF-LO, 1976.

Berman, K. V. *Comparative productivity in worker-managed co-operative plywood plants and conventionally run plants.* Unpublished paper. Washington State University, 1976.

Biderman, A. D., and Drury, T. F. *Measuring work quality for social reporting.* Halsted Press, 1976.

Birchall, D., and Wild, R. "Autonomous work groups". *Journal of General Management,* Autumn 1974, pp. 36-43.

Björk, Lars E. "An experiment in work satisfaction". *Scientific American,* Mar. 1975, pp. 17-23.

Blauner, Robert. *Alienation and freedom: The factory worker and his industry.* University of Chicago Press, 1964.

Brossard, M., and Maurice, M. "Is there a universal model of organization structure?" *International Studies of Management and Organization* (1976), pp. 11-45.

British Oxygen Company Ltd. Unpublished paper by the Manpower Development Unit, 1971.

Burns, Tom, and Stalker, G. M. *The management of innovation.* London, Tavistock Publications, 1961.

Butera, F. "Environmental factors in job and organization design: The case of Olivetti". In L. E. Davis and A. B. Cherns (eds.): *The quality of working life* (The Free Press, 1975), Vol. 2.

Butteriss, M., and Murdoch, R. D. *Work restructuring projects and experiments in the United Kingdom,* Report No. 2, Work Research Unit, United Kingdom Department of Employment, 1975.

— *Work restructuring projects and experiments in the United States of America,* Report No. 3, Work Research Unit, United Kingdom Department of Employment, 1976.

Chartrand, Phillip J. "The impact of organization on labour relations at Air Canada". *The Canadian Personnel and Industrial Relations Journal,* Jan. 1976, pp. 22-26.

Cotgrove, Stephen; Dunham, Jack; and Namplew, Clive. *The nylon spinners: A case study in productivity bargaining and job enlargement.* London, Allen and Unwin, 1971.

Cox, David, and Sharp, K. M. Dyce. "Research on the unit of work". *Occupational Psychology.* Apr. 1951, pp. 90-108.

Cummings, T. G., and Salipante, P. F. "Research-based strategies for improving work life". In P. Warr (ed.): *Personal goals and work design* (Wiley, 1976), pp. 31-41.

Davis, L. E. "Toward a theory of job design". *Journal of Industrial Engineering,* Sep.-Oct. 1957, pp. 305-307.

Davis, L. E., and Cherns, A. B. (eds.). *The quality of working life.* The Free Press, 1975.

Donnelly, J. F. "Increasing productivity by involving people in their total job". *Personnel Administrator,* Sep.-Oct. 1971.

Edstrom, A. *User influence on the development of MIS: A contingency approach.* Unpublished working paper, European Institute for Advanced Studies in Management, Brussels, 1976.

Edwards, G. A. B. *Readings in group technology.* The Machinery Publishing Co., 1971.

Epple, D.; Fidler, E.; and Goodman, P. *Estimating economic consequences in organizational effectiveness experiments.* Unpublished working paper, Carnegie-Mellon University, Pittsburgh, n.d.

Fitzroy, F. R., and Hiller, J. R. *Efficiency and motivation in productive organizations.* Discussion paper, International Institute of Management, Berlin, 1978.

Flamholtz, E. G. *Human asset accounting.* Dickenson, 1974.

Galbraith, John Kenneth. *Economics and the public purpose.* Boston, Houghton Mifflin, 1973.

Green, J. M. (ed.). *Production and inventory control handbook.* McGraw-Hill, 1970.

Gustafson, H. W. *Force-loss cost analysis.* Paper presented to the AWV-Fachseminar: "Das Humankapital der Unternehmen", Bonn, September 1974.

Hepworth, A., and Osbaldeston, M. *Restructuring the motor insurance section.* Ashridge Management College Research Unit, 1975.

Herrick, N. Q. *The quality of work and its outcomes: Estimating potential increases in labor productivity.* Academy for Contemporary Problems, Ohio, 1975.

den Hertog, J. F. *Work structuring.* Eindhoven, Philips, 1974.

— *Work system design: Experiences with alternative production organizations.* Eindhoven, Philips, 1976.

Hill, Paul. *Towards a new philosophy of management: The company development programme of Shell UK Limited.* London, Gower Press, 1971.

Huse, Edgar F., and Beer, Michael. "Eclectic approach to organizational development". *Harvard Business Review,* Sep.-Oct. 1971, pp. 103-112.

Jenkins, David. *Job power: Blue and white collar democracy.* New York, Doubleday, 1973.

— *Industrial democracy in Europe* Business International, 1974.

Jonson, L. C.; Jönsson, B.; and Svensson, G. "The application of social accounting to absenteeism and personnel turnover". *Accounting, Organisations and Society,* Vol. 3 (1979), Nos. 3-4.

Kenton, Leslie. "The seven year switch". *Industrial Management* (London), May 1973. pp. 14-19.

Klein, Lisl. *New forms of work organization.* Cambridge University Press, 1976.

Kornhauser, A. *Mental health of the industrial worker.* New York, John Miller Press, 1965.

Latham, G. P., and Pursell, E. D. "Measuring absenteeism from the opposite side of the coin". *Journal of Applied Psychology,* 1975, pp. 369-371.

Lawler, Edward E., III. "Job design and employee motivation". *Personnel Psychology,* Vol. 22, 1969, pp. 426-435. Reprinted in Victor H. Vroom and Edward L. Deci (eds.): *Management and motivation,* selected readings (Harmondsworth, Middlesex, Penguin Books, 1970), pp. 160-169.

— *Measuring the human organization.* Unpublished paper presented to the Human Resource Accounting Seminar, Bonn, 1974.

— "Conference review: Issues of understanding". In P. Warry (ed.): *Personal goals and work design* (Wiley, 1976), pp. 225-234.

Lawrence, Paul ⌐ Lorsch, Jay W. *Organization and environment: Managing differentiation and integre* ton, Graduate School of Business Administration, Harvard University, 1967.

Lemaire, B. "Comptes de surplus et économie de transition". *Revue Française de Gestion,* Sep. 1977, pp. 18-23.

Likert, Rensis. *The human organization: Its management and value.* New York, McGraw-Hill, 1967.

Lindestad, H., and Kvist, A. *The Volkswagen Report.* Swedish Employers' Confederation, 1975.

Locke, E. A. "The nature and causes of job satisfaction". In M. D. Dunnette (ed.): *Handbook of industrial and organizational psychology* (Rand-McNally, 1976).

Lutz, B. "Bildungssystem und Beschäftigungsstruktur in Deutschland und Frankreich". In H. G. Mendivs et. al.: *Betrieb-Arbeitsmarkt-Qualifikation,* 1 (Frankfurt, Aspekte Verlag, 1976).

Macy, Barry A., and Mirvis, Philip H. "A methodology for assessment of quality of work life and organizational effectiveness in behaviorial-economic terms". *Administrative Science Quarterly,* June 1976, pp. 212-226.

Maher, John; Overbagh, Wayne; Palmer, Gerald; and Piersol, Darrell. "Enriched jobs improve inspection". *Work Study and Management Services,* Oct. 1970, pp. 821-824.

Maître, P. "The measurement of the creation and distribution of wealth in a firm by the method of surplus accounts". *Accounting, Organizations and Society*, Vol. 3 (1979), Nos. 3-4.

Manufacturing Management, December 1972. "Work teams at Pye beat production line problems".

Maurice, M.; Sorge, A.; and Warner, M. *Societal differences in organizing manufacturing units: A comparison of France, West Germany and Great Britain*. Paper presented to the Ninth Congress of Sociology, Upsala, 1978.

Melman, S. "Managerial versus co-operative decision making in Israel". *Studies in Comparative International Development*, Vol. VI (1970-71), No. 3, pp. 47-58.

Midlands Tomorrow (West Midlands Economic Planning Council), No. 8, 1975. "Industrial productivity: Scope for improvement".

Mirvis, Philip H., and Berg, D. N. *Failures in organization development and change: Cases and essays for learning*. Wiley, 1978.

Mirvis, Philip H., and Edward E. Lawler III. "Measuring the financial impact of employee attitudes". *Journal of Applied Psychology*, Vol. 62, No. 1, 1977, pp. 1-8.

Mirvis, Philip H., and Macy, Barry A. "Accounting for the costs and benefits of human resource development programs: An interdisciplinary approach". *Accounting, Organizations and Society*, Vol. 1, Nos. 2-3, pp. 179-194.

Mott, P. E. *Shift work: The social, psychological and physical consequences*. Ann Arbor, Michigan, Institute for Social Research, 1975.

National Economic Development Office (United Kingdom). *Why group technology?* 1975.

New, C. C. *Managing manufacturing operations: A survey of current practice in 186 plants*. British Institute of Management, 1976.

Norstedt, Jan-Peder, and Agurén, Stefán. *The Saab-Scania report: Experiment with modified work organizations and work forms: Final report*. Stockholm, Swedish Employers' Confederation, 1973.

Paul, W. J., and Robertson, C. B. *Job enrichment and employee motivation*. Gower Press, 1970.

Portigal, A. H. (ed.). *Measuring the quality of working life*. Information Canada, 1974.

— *Towards the measurement of work satisfaction*. OECD Social Indicator Development Programme Special Studies No. 1. Paris, Organisation for Economic Co-operation and Development, 1976.

Powers, R. *An empirical investigation of selected hypotheses related to the success of management information system projects*. Unpublished Ph.D. dissertation, University of Minnesota, 1972.

Price, J. L. *The correlates of turnover*. Department of Sociology, University of Iowa, Working Paper No. 73-1.

Ranson, G. H. *Group technology*. McGraw-Hill, 1972.

Salter, W. E. G. *Productivity and technical change*. Cambridge University Press, Second edition, 1969.

Schoderbeck, P., and Rief, W. *Job enlargement*. Ann Arbor, Michigan, University of Michigan Press, 1969.

Schon, Donald A. *Beyond the stable state: Public and private learning in a changing society*. Temple Smith, 1971.

Seashore, S. E. "Assessing the quality of working life". *Labour and Society*, Apr. 1976, pp. 69-80.

Sirota, David, and Wolfson, Alan D. "Job enrichment". *Personnel* (Saranac Lake, New York, American Management Association), May-June 1972, pp. 8-17, and July-Aug. 1972, pp. 8-19.

Smith, Adam. *Wealth of nations*.

Spooner, P. "Group technology gives Platt a smoother run". *Business Administration*, Apr. 1973.

Srivastva, S., et al. *Productivity, industrial organization and job satisfaction: Policy development and implementation*. Report to the National Science Foundation. Case Western Reserve University, 1975.

Staehle, Wolfgang H. "Federal Republic of Germany". In Vol. 1 of the present work, pp. 77-106.

Swanson, B. "Management information systems: Appreciation and involvement". *Management Science*, 1974.

Taylor, J. C., et al. *The quality of working life: An annotated bibliography, 1957-1972.* Center for Organizational Studies, Graduate School of Management, University of California, Los Angeles, 1972.

Taylor, J. C. "Experiments in work system design: Economic and human results". *Personel Review,* Summer 1977, pp. 21-34, and Autumn 1977, pp. 21-42.

Taylor, L. K. *Not for bread alone: An appreciation of job enrichment.* Business Books, Second edition, 1973.

— *A fairer slice of the cake: The task ahead.* Business Books, 1975.

Templé, P. "La méthode des surplus: Un essai d'application aux comptes des entreprises, 1959-1967". *Economie et Statistique,* 1971, pp. 33-50.

Tuggle, G. "Job enlargement: An assault on assembly line inefficiencies". *Industrial Engineering,* Feb. 1969, pp. 26-31.

Ulich, E. "Die Erweitung des Handlungsspielraumes in der betrieblichen Praxis". *Industrielle Organisation,* Vol. 43 (1974), No. 1.

United Nations. *Methods of determining social allocations.* Report of the Secretary-General to the Sixteenth Session of the Social Commission of the Economic and Social Council. United Nations document E/CN.5/387, 31 Mar. 1965.

Van Der Merwe, R., and Miller, Sylvia. "The measurement of labour turnover: A critical appraisal and a suggested new approach". *Human Relations,* June 1971, pp. 233-253.

Vanek, Jaroslav. *The general theory of labor-managed economies.* Ithaca, New York, Cornell University Press, 1970.

— *The participatory economy: An evolutionary hypothesis and a strategy for development.* Ithaca, New York, Cornell University Press, 1971.

Walters, R. *Job enrichment for results.* Addison-Wesley, 1975.

Walton, R. E. *Workplace alteration and the need for major innovation.* Unpublished paper, 1972.

Weil, Reinhold. *Alternative forms of work organisation: Improvements of labour conditions and productivity in Western Europe.* International Institute for Labour Studies, Research Series, No. 4. Geneva, 1976.

Weir, M. *Redesigning jobs in Scotland: A survey.* Work Research Unit Report No. 5. United Kingdom Department of Employment, 1976.

Wilkinson, A. *A survey of some Western European experiments in motivation.* Institute of Work Study Practitioners, 1970.

Williamson, D. T. N. "The anachronistic factory". *Proceedings of the Royal Society,* Series A, 1972, pp. 139-160.

Woodruff, R. L. *Accounting for human research costs.* Paper presented at the AWV-Fachseminar on "Das Humankapital der Unternehmen", Bonn, 1974.

Work in America. Report of a special task force to the Secretary of Health, Education and Welfare, prepared under the auspices of the W. E. Upjohn Institute for Employment Research. Cambridge, Massachusetts, MIT Press, 1972.